THE COMING OF THE THIRD WORLD AND OTHER FABLE

A Collection of Short Stories, Poetry, and Essays

by George Langston Cook

I0192389

Published by George Langston Cook
Phoenix, AZ

i

Published by George Langston Cook
Phoenix, Arizona 2009
Printed in the USA

Table of Contents

SHORT STORY SECTION (49)

MY JOURNEY SECTION (91)

Forward

This collection includes my mostly unpublished writings. Most of my stories and poems have sat on decaying paper for years, unseen but not forgotten, only distributed in one form of another to friends. One poem "Someone I Once Knew" was once submitted by one of those friends to the International Library of Poetry where it was published in their compilation "A Falling Star" under my name in 2001.

Some things will remain unreleased in this publication; short essays and social documentary pieces such as "The New Nigger" and "State of the Union" that are extremely dated to the time in which they were written. I also left out articles I wrote for "The ECCO", the junior college newspaper of Essex County College I wrote for and edited while a student there.

I am hoping that what I do present here actually transcend time, provoke thought, and are enjoyable. Thank you.

George Langston Cook
January 2009

Dedication

I thank the times in which I have lived, the people whom I have known, and the wonders I have seen in my travels. They all contributed to the production of this work. I combined both my cynicisms and hopes within in an attempt to enlighten you and aid the rediscovery of your own social consciousness and a sense of morality.

I acknowledge my experiences growing up in the Christopher Columbus Homes of Newark, New Jersey. The memory of people from those projects brings me both great joy and immense pain. They keep me in touch with the belief that all people possess positive character values, despite the outcome of their lives.

I thank a seventh grade teacher, Miss Kiernan, for claiming I copied the first poem I ever wrote from somebody named Longfellow. I also credit a friend from that same class, Ms. Lynn Janifer, for inspiring me to write. She stated the letters I wrote to her visually described my thoughts, moods, and surrounding.

I thank the U.S. Navy for being there when I needed to mature away from Newark. Through the military, I was able to see the world, and begin to express my longings with the pen. While serving, I expanded my knowledge of myself and avoided many of the downfalls suffered by a number of my childhood peers.

Essex County College's Student Activities Department provided me with the first formal outlet for my writing ability. At Arizona State University, I made lifelong friends who encouraged my expressions of social awareness.

I dedicate my work to my late parents who fostered my love of knowledge, and provided a fertile home life in which my talents grew. And I thank God for blessing me with the confidence to proceed with this project.

George Langston Cook
May 2001

Introduction

The stories and poetry contained within this anthology crystallize how one person envisions the problems of his time. You may ask, "What gives this writer, who possibly possesses only marginal social perceptions, the right to judge the morals of this society? Are his perceptions real?"

What is real anyway? It I base reality only on my senses, what exists if I close my eyes and refuse to accept all other sensory inputs? The answer is nothing besides myself, for to confirm my own being takes only my conscious mind. I know only that I exist. Yet, when I open my eyes, a world appears beside me.

You may also ask, "What are the grounds on which I stand?" If in my blindness I assume the position of standing on whatever grounds my mind wills there, then, that is my intellectual prerogative. It is within the power of the individual to believe what he wants to.

In America, I believe there is something wrong with how people deal with ones' self and each other. We have poor communication with our inner self. We fail to identify and acknowledge our natural instincts. We think something evil creates them. We blame what we feel and think on what occurs outside of our being.

Dishonesty, fear, greed, and resentment dominate many of our relationships. We base our love on the ability to provide creature comforts or to satisfy our animal lusts. If we perceive even the slightest difference between others and ourselves, war breaks out.

Our institutions are bent on obtaining and maintaining control over our behavior. We fuel them with dollars rather than with the mission to perform the greatest good for the greatest number. Our schools have become like prisons, and our homes like isolation wards.

P.S. I have but one consolation for the world in which we live. I believe in God, and I know He will see us through.

George Langston Cook
August 1983

Poetry Section

Sometimes it's in the rhythm,
sometimes it's in the rhyme
Most often it's in feelings and thoughts
that run on the backroads of my mind

George Langston Cook
June 13, 2009

No Small Thing
(A Morning Prayer of Love)

It's no small thing

but as easy to hide

this feeling of love

I keep buried inside.

It's no small thing

but as hard to see

the feeling i have

for you hold its key.

It's no small thing

once more I'll say

this love, this love, and me

are yours to have each day.

I hope you enjoy my book

Who is In the Driver's Seat?

Oh my Lord, I'm on my knees
please hear the prayer I pray.
Oh Lord, your help I need
and your word I will obey.

You are in the driver's seat
and always in control.
You command my heart beat
and orchestrate my soul.

My life march on at a quickening pace
for what, nobody knows.
I thought it all to be a race
and ran where no one goes.

In me it created anarchy
and all others I tried to defeat.
It took away my harmony
and turned up the dag blamed heat.

So help me Lord to find my peace
to make a difference with my life.
Help me live a life with feasts
instead a one with strife.

Prayer

this life seems to have played a terrible trick on me
birthing me generations too early or centuries too late
as I trudge slowly along its darkened and lonely path
wondering always if this life was meant to be my fate

the beat downs, the put downs, and the many defeats
overshadow brief moments of joy in my life that I see
it's my fault, you know, having the shadow of the veil
to be able to bring joy to others but can't make it in me

I am hurting, Oh Lord, I am hurting real bad
I know you Almighty God above have a plan
to raise my spirits through this darkened time
so that I can lift my head and take a stand

now all around me the walls start closing in fast
I'm in training for what seems my greatest fight
I won't give in Lord, I just won't let them win
I'll fight my demons and drag them screaming into the light

Thoughts

Many things have been going

through my mind lately

Most of them have to do

with my relationships with others

I find myself in a confused state

in terms of these relationships

when I believe I have given my all

I have been taking

taking people's precious time

to feed my ego

and giving in return only

my inflated pride

I was too blind to see this

while all the time wondering why

I've not gotten from my associations

what I desired

It's time for a change

To Myself

I seem always
to be down and out
but I never really
know why.
And just when things seem
dreary and dark
I'll look at me and smile.
I'll say I get the impression
that people do like me
for things that I myself
truly can not see.
And this is when
I'll stop and think
that even I like me

(stranger things have been known to happen)

Visions

We all have visions and dreams
of what we'd like to see or feel.
I am not different in that respect.
When and if these things occur
we take it almost as a blessing.
but me, once I dream
I expect it to come true
and if it does not
in a reasonable length of time
then I have a job to do.
To make these visions into reality
may require you to work on yours
as I work on mine,
all except for the fact
my strongest vision
is that we worked together.
That is why I'm here.

Ever

Ever try to catch a dream
to put an image in your mind
or do you find you've no control
over things and over time

Ever try to make a wish
then see that it comes true
or never hoping, never caring
whether or not they do

Ever look for peace of mind
in the life you live
There's no need to look much further
for that's my wish to give

Don't worry about tomorrow
for yes – the sun will rise
Don't worry about the life you live
for it's only a disguise

Don't worry about those wishes
or the images on the mind,
for you will never know
whose dreams you'll help to find

Search for peace, you'll find it
everywhere you look
Believe me and be strong people
a poem by George Langston Cook

The Dream

I once had a dream
in which I slipped and fell
but never touched the ground

I was like an airplane
no, a drifting eagle
floating through the air, effortlessly

the winds moved my body
my mind controlled
the way I went
and I soared higher
higher than the tallest buildings
higher than man has gone before
without assistance

I touched the stars
and I loved the feeling
as if it were something
you could never really truly know

To fly like a bird
to come and go freely
and I did it all

In the dream I wished
that when I awoke
it would all happen again
but this time – in no dream

Have You Ever Been Lonely

Have you ever cried
because no one was there
no one who matters,
no one who cares
have you ever been lonely

Have you ever needed to be loved
and no one was there
no one to hold on to,
when your eyes held back the tears
have you ever been lonely

What you feel is nothing new
it happens to us all sometime
you must always be ready
for everything will be fine

So whatever you do-please remember
you really have nothing to fear
because you'll never be lonely
just as long as I am near.

For I have been so lonely
I did not want to live
though my heart was full of love
there was no one that love I could give.

Just let me be near you
just spend some time with me
then you'll never be lonely again
and we'll be happy just wait and see.

Am I Listening?
Did I Hear You?

Early dusk, facing East toward the mountain, the camel's hump catching the last beams of yellow, as elsewhere purple begins to drop down from the heavens, and two multicolored archways of prism light appear from out of nowhere.

The sight brought hope and courage to my soul, pre-cursing the invitation to dinner, a chance, an opportunity to spend time to impress you with a hand prepared meal warm music good food, just to get to know you.

Small talk questions and answers, and small talk some more, a moment of laughter, a smile, then a glance, then words followed by a bite and sip of sauce.

Time passed slowly and too quickly we looked across the table at each other endlessly

Speaking, I did the most of I'm sure, putting my foot in my mouth more often than I care to admit.

Seeking not to say what I wanted to, for that would be putting all my cards on the table, and I fear that losing.

You listened and I watched your face

Your eyes are beautiful almonds, and upon looking into them, a pain appeared to me.

Was I listening or just observing my own soul's reflection coming from the depths of your soulful stare?

You spoke of pain from youth years spent, pent up anger, misplace love, and yet un-cynically you profess yourself to be not alone but by yourself, with friends but to yourself.

And then you asked if I was listening.

To the silence of our eyes, and to the beat of our hearts, to the rise of your breast, with every deep or shallow breath, to the words of from your throat, to the sounds the come from inside, thinking of how we will spend our silent time together; of the hours of kiss, and the moments of bliss, of the cry of our hearts, and as we sigh.

I thought for days how to respond

Am I listening?

And I wonder if it is most important whether I listened to you or not, as long as I heard you.

Trees Are Like Men

look at the trees
how their limbs are
bent over by the wind
Weighed down by ice and snow
of a cold wet winter

They remind me of the spirits
of downhearted broken men
each one wears its own bends
just like people who have a look
special only to themselves

maybe in another time
maybe past, maybe future
trees were or will be men

maybe even now
trees are like men

fruitful when conditions permit
barren in the cold
almost like men
when they are young or old

Trees are Men

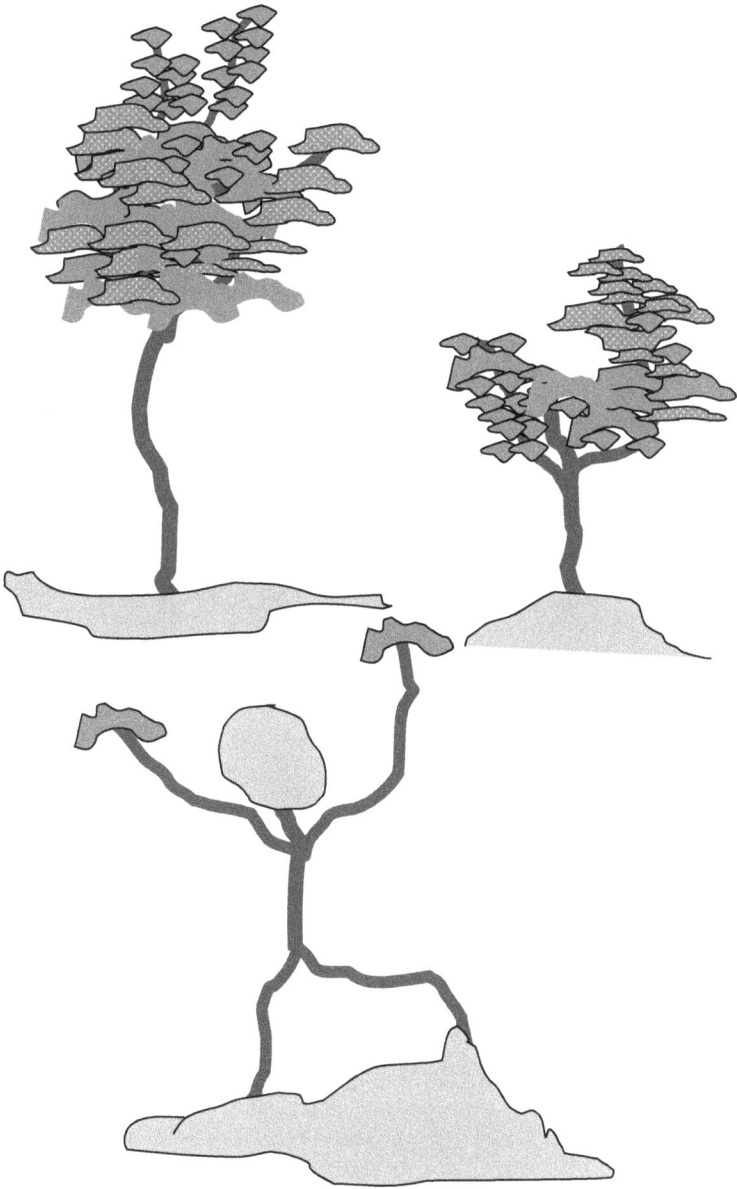

What You Really Did

Did you ever really try
to give respect
to all your Black brothers and sisters?

And did you in the process get used
for their own no good purposes?

Then what you really did
was not respect and understand
the way they are
but have only said
in your heart
that they are only Niggers.

Really!

and they heard you

A Little Something for the Homeboys

I.

Poor young homey
lying there dead
Never thought to hear
what older folk said

He thought he had the answers
and always talked about crime
He acted like a tough guy
'til the judge gave him the time

He made everybody fear him,
he just had to be cool
And he didn't even care
when he dropped out of school

His work was pulling stick ups
his fun was doing drugs
Til the day they found his body
laying face down in the mud

The homey had a problem-
the life he had was sad
And the way his parents raised him-
the boy just had it bad

They beat him when they wanted to,
and then they left him all alone
And then when he was just thirteen
he started getting stoned

When he should have gone to high school
instead he just got high
And then when he was sixteen
he caused someone to die

Revenge and hatred chased him
and one day they both caught up
And that is how we found him,
shot, and stabbed and throat cut

II

Sallie is a dreamer
He lives his life in fantasy
He thinks he is a rapper
But he can't do it style free

If he wants to be remembered
He would have to do these three
Do his work and keep it down
And live more in reality

III

I'd be a better rapper
If I had a better rhyme
I'd do it even better
If I only had the time
I'd love it for the millions
But I'd do it for a dime
So it's okay for me my brother
For this day will turn out fine

IV

To be a better rapper
You have got to know the rules
You have to know the language arts
That they teach you here in school
And then if you come to master them
Your raps will sound real cool
And you would be the man someday
Instead of a boy cleaning pools

Stig Mo Tized

That is my name … Stig Mo Tized

see me accepting slaps

on the back of my own head

calling myself names no one else can pronounce

told I can do no more than

talk bad english…fail in school…get hooked on drugs…

go to jail…without passing go…no payday

play basketball…run like hell…quit the game of life

fight the will of God…

engage in sweat producing fornication all night

to make other little brothers and sisters

all possessing traumatized attributes

just like me…

escape responsibilities of caring for them

steal their legacies

then before the age of twenty five…

die violently.

Where does it end? What do I win?

not here, not now, not a thing

the system can't let me in, won't let me in…

all excuses work…I don't

positive motivation eludes me

positive contributions escape me

they really fear me

and see me as too much a threat

so I am left alone as a bloated carcass

rats and roaches feast on me in my sleep

and the rotting stench from my empty life fills my abode

I am pathetic…alone…and traumatized

Lost in a world not of my own making

Stig Mo Tized

Someone I Once Knew

As life moves nearer to uncertain ends
and the catching of names in notices begins
accomplishments and associations mass
when the sums of human existence pass

From commonly shared experience
intersecting lives and remembrance
frequent heartaches together we cried
songs we sang forever survived

Friend, family, associate,
lover, neighbor, compatriot
we closely bonded brothers once
let time and distance separate us

now the words of character traits declare
and describe the one I once held dear
whose recent demise raises feelings anew
and praise the memory of someone I once knew

Lisa

I saw Lisa for the first time in years
And to see her this way brought me to tears

She once was so gifted, and so full of life
Now she battles her mind's inner strife

I want to blame God for what I deplore
How her mind has left her abandoned and poor

Who would have thought this young girl so glad
Would be living her middle life out of a bag

Not knowing or caring how she did charm
While her mind says old friends are out to do harm

I have not been able to sleep all night
My memories of her begin to lose their light

What I have now is a reality so stark
That a beautiful mind can't escape its own dark

There's a Cold Wind

There's a cold wind a blowin'
hard up against the wall
It's a cold breeze
it seeps through the cracks
and touches me on the other side

There's a cold wind a blowin'
hard up against the wall
It freezes all that moves
dead in its tracks
and touches me on the other side

There's a cold wind a blowin'
hard up against the wall
Sister, hold your breath
warm your cold heart
and that cold wind will subside

Pretty Flowers

When you walk through the garden of life
there is nothing wrong in stopping
to appreciate the flowers along the way.

Even to pick one for your lapel
or a bunch for your table
is something that will give great pleasure
for a long time.

But to trample through the garden
not caring for the beauty of the flowers
and to cut them down
only because they are there
is like the destruction of the family
and love itself.

Every young woman in love is like a pretty flower
who is willing to open her petals
and give away her wondrous scent and nectar.

To abuse that love, to destroy that flower
is to make the world less beautiful
the woman less trusting
for those who come after

In a Dream

last night I was awaken by a nice dream
of being with a beautiful Nubian queen
together we met in a familiar scene
but her face was one I never have seen

oh how I would hope to meet this day
a dark-skinned lovely with a young woman's way
a bounce in her step while her hips slightly sway
and only positive things would she ever have to say

she took me to meet her parents at her house
they sat together watching TV on the couch
they seemed happy that I had happened about
I spoke with them until she came back out

a different outfit now she did wear
the vision of her was so easy to bear
and with her she carried two folding chairs
I guess that she wanted me to be near

I felt happy and I loved to look at her face
and I felt comfortable around her place
mutual attraction seemed to be more the case
and the dream seemed not to be a race

it was at this moment from the dream I awoke
and wondered why on me was played this joke
that I would be surrounded by such nice folk
and the lovely Nubian Queen of whom I spoke

as I think of this dream I ponder upon
that this Nubian queen's image was so strong
I wonder what in my life that I'd done wrong
that for me real love has been away too long

and that the only way for me to find it is in a dream

It's Real

Fire
life dancing through old pine logs
popping fingers excitingly

Warm
flickering light
subtle colors
sensed by the blind
the dumb
and the lame

Loving
translucent
blue glow

Red
felt with closed eyes

It sings
it's there
low humming
gentle breezes
barely audible

A heartbeat
known by its pressure
on your eardrums

Bubbling, gurgling laughter

The flame
smooth, soothing calm
tranquilizing
hypnotizing
tauntingly mesmerizing
holding transfixed
in place in time
embracing without touching
forever

Your love

Am I Paranoid

am I paranoid to think
there is a good reason
post interview phone calls
are not being returned or answered
even after I am told to
expect an offer within a few days
when I call the cell phones
and offices of human resources
interviewers and company officials.

am I paranoid to think
the world is out against me
is there some terrible master plan
to see my pride falter and fall
is it that my human destruction
may be at hand.

am I paranoid to think
they don't want me to think
just follow without questioning
to find answers to questions they ignore
to actually know why I must do
what I must do
more than they tell me.

am I paranoid to think
my foresight and insight
the work I have done
for nearly two decades
is no longer valued
that the kind of person I am
with the personality I have
is of no value
despite the skills I show
with my clients
that I am satisfied with me
and they are not.

am I paranoid to think
I am black
and have been
black-balled

Winter

tingling feelings replace normal nothingness of toes
as each foot hits the rock hard pavement
frozen since the Nordic express
and clear blue skies
railroaded its way into the city
with winds faster than a speeding bullet
and colder than ice
no snow fell

blowing exhaled breath through woolen gloves
as a gesture to fingers long numbed
with shoulders tightly shrugged
and head tilted forward
bracing itself against falling backwards
from the force of razor sharp frigid blasts of air
that come from everywhere
it can't be blocked

inside it takes time to become warm again
the body shakes from cold withdrawal
as it lovingly embraces the heat
from the open doored oven
and pots of water boil up white vapors
that sticks to the windows as a watery mist
that runs down like rain
before it freezes

imagination has the storm trooper like cold
infiltrating the home through cracks
reaching through flesh and bone
of those living alone
this winter exist only in tortured minds
and touches all weary worn out lonely souls
living in sun-drenched and warm
sunbelt states

Questions

It is one of those days when I question myself
I have a quandary that is causing me mental pain
for uncertain am I of the path I should take
and what should I give up in order for me to gain

Now many whom are not sure of what I believe
will begin here to tell me have faith this day
that God will begin to provide me guidance
and the only thing I must do is pray

But I also know that the devil has his tricks
that often comes in a truthful disguise
so where I am at with these horrible decisions
is how to know which ones are the lies

I have in my life been fooled a lot
by those whose have deciphered me in a fashion
I have allowed them to take advantage of me
and allowed them to discount my passion

So today I have been brought to this point
and I ponder in which way I should go
should I follow my heart or follow my head
which is best, I really do not know

I am told that if I lead with my heart
if I put it on my sleeve for all to see
that people of ill will can derail my feelings
and do all that they can to hurt me

I am also told if I lead with my head
that I appear to the others as too bold
and turn off the people who might have heard what I say
and appear to be barren, hard, and cold

so which road shall I take to find happiness
shall I take the way of the head or the heart
that is why I stand at this fork in the road
because I have trouble telling each way apart

Lover's Prayer

good morning, or is it good night
what can I say to you to make you feel alright
what must I do to bring you within my sight
and what does it take to hold you tight

it is nearing the dawn of another day
and I want you to take the words I say
when I whisper in your ear and my sky turns gray
so you light my sky with sun like rays

I want to know and to understand
what you want from me to be your man
must I lift your feet from the burning sand
or show my love for you is part of my plan

there is much from you that I need for me
your shoulder to lean on to help me see
that your love for me will hold the key
of peace and happiness, eternally

Clyde

forget about Michael, Oscar, or Magic to Kareem
Earl the Pearl, Jerry West, or Dean the Dream
if I have to pick one guard to have on my team
I'd pick Clyde for he is the best guard I've seen

each year there are guards that you know can score
and there those who pass out assists even more
but Clyde brought a style to the basketball floor
and gave me memories of a game I truly adore

he played the game with a most casual flair
while the vines he wore were indeed debonair
a ball hawk whose skills were beyond compare
and whose legend I'd like to speak on here

the man when he played he was definitely cool
and would make his adversaries feel like a fool
for they could not guard him as a general rule
or stop his accurate hesitation jump shot tool

the parts of the game where he was simply the best
he played b-ball like Bobby Fischer played chess
he'd take a foul on a shot that went in with finesse
and score on that foul shot that made Marv yell "Yes"

he could be like the Pearl and scored aplenty
but he stayed real close to an average of twenty
he gave out assists just as if they were money
and pulled down rebounds like it was funny

he's the man in all the game I'd want on the floor
if the other team thought they were going to score
he'd steal the ball as the home crowd would roar
Defense, defense and Clyde would do it some more

I remember when a Bullets guard named Chenier
knocked down Clyde with a punch to Clyde's ear
Clyde sat on the floor, then without anger or tear
Then scored 44 on Phil for his high game that year

surely you remember when Willis pulled up lame
in the third quarter of that championship series game
the Lakers thought they could win when in Clyde came
and destroyed their confidence and insured his fame

and then came game seven and the Lakers found fear
when Willis came out to sounds of thunderous cheers
he stepped on to the court and encouraged his peers
then Clyde played one of his best games of that year

I was glad to see Clyde do Knick play by play
and listen to the analysis of the players of this day
he uses humor and big words in what he does say
and has no problems in telling he colors his gray

and the man still looks like he could play

Poker is Not a Sport

When I get home I am such a grouch
til I sit down on my cozy comfy couch
then I place myself in a kind of a crouch
to relax everything that makes me say ouch.

On the job all day where I did my best
shuffling paper and ink at the boss man's behest
to be left alone now is my only request
it's time for me to get some good clean rest.

On the couch is where I'll sit to eat
and I'll give myself all kinds of treats
like a sandwich made with lots of meat
and cheese that makes it oh so sweet.

The really cool part I think this is hip
is when I do somersaults and maybe a flip
without dropping a single potato chip
except for into my favorite dip.

Then I begin the search for what's on t.v.
there's a sci-fi thriller I might want to see
or perhaps a sit com or a cartoon maybe
but there is something more special to me.

Football, basketball, all athletic games
where the contestants go through physical pain
and at the end of play they'll get riches and fame
and as world champions they will get to reign.

Watching them run and toil and sweat
as they volley tennis balls over the net
or using a move you had not seen yet
while losing becomes their only regret.

But now something new I enter in these annals
as I turn to many of the sports only channels
sitting at tables instead of hunting in flannels
are people holding cards hunched over like camels.

Oh no no no no no no no no no
please tell me what I see just ain't so
that these poker players are getting all the dough
while traditional sports lose their on the air show.

At first a mistake I thought this all had to be
but this game poker has taken over many a tv
as people play a lot of poker for all the money
and the stations don't care if this I hate to see.

What's even worse if anything can be
poker is taken over everything I can see
from sports and sports talk shows on t.v.
to channels that played my best shows daily.

So what has happened to the sportsmen of old
who competed with each other body and soul
and the winner receiving medallions of gold
and walking with chests out feelin' mighty bold?

Have they injured their good throwing shoulders
or played too long games that made them older
or lost the step that made them much slower
or have they all learned to play poker?

I think the situation is getting pretty bad
and the whole darn thing is making me mad
the lack of real sports makes me feel kinda sad
and makes me want super powers I wish I had.

So I would take this whole matter to court
and as the plaintiff I would file a tort
and as the judge of this mess I'd report
to people everywhere poker is not a sport.

And to games of old I'd return the time
and poker I'd turn into a crime
so after work once again I'd unwind
and regain my after work peace of mind.

News From the Home Front

Babies are being born
and old friends die
It's often hard to know
when to laugh or when to cry

the holidays have come
and Chicago's under ice
you know the hawk off the lake
cuts through like a knife

the Bulls without Michael
are like Marines without a gun
they can still win games
but it's more work than fun

someone took pictures
and in albums they are stored
to show them to you
when you get home from war

here in the southwest
it's a bit chilly this time of year
68 during the mid-day
sunny, no wind, and sky clear.

a good classic sci-fi movie
comes on in just a little bit
you remember Forbidden Planet
it's better than many modern hits

I'll watch it, clean my house
before I fix my breakfast treat
it'll be grits, eggs, and sausage
that's what I'm gonna eat

before I left my bed though
I did what's most important today
I thought about this sister in Baghdad
and for her safe return home I did pray

Weather of the Soul

today where I live
it was 78 degrees
the sky was blue
there hardly was a breeze

the weather here's nice
but I've been where
it's cold as ice
when the sky is clear

I know of the hawk
with razor sharp claws
that cuts through clothing
without much pause

more than the weather
I write of the heart
about life that is lonely
and breaks souls apart

and like I know of
winter weather there
I also know empty
lonely days living here

Remember the Good Things

eating fried chicken with your fingers
licking an icing coated spoon clean
the kiss of a loved one that still lingers
and remembering a beautiful winter scene

strolling unguarded down home town streets
watching the people you care for smile
running just because of who you will meet
and watching an orange sky sunset for awhile

trading monopoly money for a boardwalk hotel
winning a hoard of pennies at pokeno
spending a love night in a highway motel
and not really caring who may know

remember all the people who love you too
for in the places and times that you find
the sights and smells that now surround you
are too harsh for your beautiful mind

Storytelling

Swarming honey bees in a nearby grove

A rabbit scurrying towards the underbrush

Ants marching along patrolling the area for fodder

Humming birds float in mid-air while prodding flowers for their nectar

Flapping wings send eyes searching skyward

Finding varieties of birds too numerous to count

The abundance of life brings peace and contentment flourishes

Communion with nature tranquilizes restless spirits and loneliness disappears

Smoothly blending parcels of neighboring country landscape

Reminiscent of large patchwork quilts constructed with various textured rags

Down the winding road rise slightly elevated mounds of green

Bordered with columns of maple and crowned with clumps of oak

Clover covered meadows surrounding springs of dandelions

Acres of corn and wheat fields dotted with an occasional farmhouse

Happy sweat soaked men toiling
in the fields reaping the harvest

Unprotected from rays of sun streaming
down out of clear blue skies

Void of turmoil

I am overwhelmed

Horror Show

Paint a picture of mankind
Do it with the blood spilled
in all his words
<u>Horror Show-Act One</u>

Write another nursery rhyme
Do it at the expense of
a character now slanted for life
<u>Horror Show – Act Two</u>

All good shows have three acts
This last one must consist of genocide
for that is the way this last act seems to be going

To Be God

What is it
that makes a man kill another?

Maybe it' because
at the actual moment
the deathblow is struck
the killer feels it's a matter
of life and death
between himself and his victim

Maybe because
he feels as if his very existence
and everything he stands for
is being threatened by the one
now within the breeches
of his manhood

But then again
it's maybe his uncontrollable desire
born and bred in the corridors
and back roads of his mind

TO BE GOD

Short Story Section

Who says fables are just for kids?

The Storyteller

I was walking along a road in a rural setting, round about late August a few years ago. Kind of nice was the day; blue skies and shade of trees. The scene seemed so full of life; green vegetation and the humming of busy insects. Peaceful and contented I felt. Alone I was but not lonely, maybe the communion with nature and country sounds tranquilized my otherwise restless soul. Winding road, trees of pine, open fields of corn and wheat, and occasional farm house in the distance. It seemed so strange! No men, women or children could I see. There should have been tan faced men soaking with the sweat earned in the fields from their toil under a baking hot sun.

Where were the people? No town nearby; no schools or churches visible. Just a notion I thought, while gazing the boundaries of earth and sky along the horizon. A sound in the distance - I strained to hear – maybe a breeze rustling the leaves, - time passes - no not a breeze, voices - youthful-laughing-joyfully. The birds flew towards me then over head and veered off towards the sound of laughter, alighting on large shade trees that hid a small clearing from view. They chirped and flirted with the sounds of oooh's and aaah's. Then there was a silence so it seemed as I approached the glen.

Around the edge clearing sat children and their mothers, teenagers, and young lovers. In the middle of that mass was an old man sitting on an old tree stump. He was speaking softly at this point. I could not hear just what still out of earshot, so moved closer found a place to sit. At

50

that point the man was building towards some climatic conclusion it seemed of some sort of tale. He was jumping and shouting. Still I couldn't understand what because I was getting tired, drowsy. Then closed mine eyes and fell asleep by a small pond then I heard and understood as long as I was sleep.

And the man raised a pointed finger to the sky, shook his head and said, "Don't let this ever happen to you." The children laughed, the young lovers and women applauded. Great joy I felt within the sleep as I too felt a stinging in the palms of my hands! I was clapping too, though I only understood the last line. "More, more" was shouted by the crowd, and I wanted too, to hear more of what the man said.

And then as I fell into deeper slumber, he began storytelling again by saying "Let me tell you now about a more serious matter. Why are there no men here?

The Answer

"Oh hell," say I when I awake for another day. It is too late to wish for death in my bed. Another day has dawned on my life, leaving me no alternative but to live it.

Every morning I wake up with the same thought. It is not that I despise the experiences that make up my life, but why in hell did they have to happen to me.

My memory takes me back to the pleasant days of growing up, Black in a white world. Everything I learned was in contradiction to itself by experience, like the days I found myself forced into attending confraternity classes. That was freaky. Imagine being seven years old and afraid of death. I didn't want to go to hell, and knew for sure I was going because I could not afford a new blue suit so I could be confirmed. Little did I know the world in which I lived was Hell in all its' glory.

Yes! Glory be to Hell, as long as I'm living here.

Those classes really had me going through a thing. Moms did not help much either, but I don't blame her for believing that religion they were selling. They almost had me believing it too, until I saw that not even God could get her out of jail. Even the priest said there was nothing he could do. He said she shouldn't have tried to cut the woman who stole my father away from the family. I punched him in the eye. He said nothing to me directly, but I heard him mumble something about a nigga boy going to Hell for all eternity. Little did he really know.

Later life experiences were no better. School was close to the worst. Since I had to go, I went. I didn't know there was no room for smart Negroes. I remember how the teachers talked about slavery. They always seemed quite happy to discuss it, but that was before the riots of '67. After that year, we were given Black teachers, and then society labeled our school system substandard.

School was hell. I enjoyed being by myself at times, but when I was, teachers beat me then sent me to their analysts. I told them all lies, and they said I was normal. I guess I fooled them.

I had a lot of fights with my peers. Fights were not fun then, and I always lost because I would not fight back. Someone told me a wise man will run away in order to live another day. I thought I was a wise man; my friends called me a fool. They were right.

It took me too long in life to respect experience; like it wasn't until the military became a part of my life before I said "stop". Religion taught me love and respect for all, family did so even more. The military taught me hate.

Before the military, I thought hate was unreal. Even when my peers beat me up daily I knew they didn't hate me. It's just that they liked beating me up more than I did. Ahh! But the military; they taught me to kill, and to hate the enemy.

For the first time in my life, I found people that could hate me for the hell of it. I'd go to sleep at night in my rack to be woken by 50 white boys trying to kill me. I still don't know why, but my being Black at that time must have been the reason, especially since none of them were. Oh hell, again and again.

Now I'm at the point in my life where I need answers. Hell sounds like a good one, and so does hate, but they don't answer the question. They don't leave much room to grow in.

The Jump

There was once a man who did not know why he lived. He questioned everything, especially his own existence. Yet, whenever he got to a point where his questions would be answered if he jumped, he refused to do so.

The first such opportunity came while he was but a child, playing a child's game with his friends, jumping over an old concrete barrel twice his height, without the use of his hands. All his friends did so with no problems what so ever, but when his turn came, he refused. He was afraid he'd slip, fall, and hurt himself.

At another time in his childhood, he witnessed the leap of a man from the top of a tall building. That man died, but our youth did not understand the meaning of that suicidal jump.

The boy grew to young adulthood, and jumped at the first opportunity he had, which was into the ocean from a fifty foot platform. He thought he could swim but if not for those around him, he would have drowned. He lived...just so that he could still question everything. He learned nothing from the experience of his foolhardy jump.

As a man, he left home again, and twice failed to jump when the opportunity arose. He was afraid, but of course, he didn't know it. He still questioned, yet understood nothing, for he did not learn from his life's experiences.

One day, quite unexpectedly, the man received a bump while playing another child's game, and he fell to the ground. It happened again and he was hurt. The strangest thing about the incident was that for the first time, the man began to understand what was happening to him. After that realization, he never fell from a bump again.

That incident shined the light of understanding onto all prior lifetime experiences, yet he still did not know what it all meant until the day he made his fateful jump.

It was an impulse, no perhaps an instinct that drove him to jump. It did not seem to matter how high he was from the ground; he just did not care. He had seen something fall from where he was to the ground, and he knew he had to save whatever it was that fell from the grace of his presence. The people around him warned him not to do it. He did not seem to hear them. He only knew what he had to do.

Without recourse, he stepped over the safety rail, stooped into a kind of a squat, took a deep breath, and let out a yell that silenced the critics. Then he jumped.

From the time he left his perch he did not once think of the consequences of his jump, yet he knew the termination of this jump would give him the answers he had desired since his birth. The story ends when the man hits the ground.

(I just had to leave him hanging.)

Hands

There was a time not long ago when the man could not find a reason why he had his hands. He used them, of course, almost every day in his life. But he did not realize their importance. This fact never occurred to him, just as many other things just passed him by.

He was a young man when he first heard that his hands were to be used to achieve the wants he had in mind to keep. He learned he'd have to hold them, so he did without paying the slightest attention as to how he did so.

He was told one way to fight was with his hands; to strike out with or to hold on to the things he struck out with. He learned his hands were potent weapons, the most deadly he could ever really need. The fear this brought him had its effect for he rarely used his hands in that capacity.

The most amazing thing he was told in his youth was that with his hands he could create. From wood, metal, cloth, and ink his hands could make a masterpiece. But this man would spurn all he had heard about the use of his hands, contributing it all to the workings of an intelligent and highly creative mind.

This man put everything into the realm of his mind's creativity, yet he failed to see this creativity as being useless without a linkage to the real world. All things for him were mental expressions, even his feelings and emotions. The man never realized that his hands were quite sensitive themselves. He did not understand their sense of touch.

We should know this could not go on forever, for all conditions are subject to change. The man, now in his mid twenties was due to find out just how and why his hands were important.

The day came when he had also learned to walk down his road, where before he barely crawled on all fours. He was crawling up a steep incline, and could not see in front beyond his nose. Despite this lack of vision, he used his hands to grab precious inches to help him along his way. In his blindness, the man reached up into the darkness, and then yelled out. He drew a hand back to find it had been bitten unmercifully by the ignorance of his mind. Seeking to throw off that excruciating feeling gripping his hand, he succeeded only in contaminating his other hand. He yelled, he screamed, and almost cried. His hands held this ungodly feeling that his mind told him was pain.

He was lost, and did not know what to do. He brought his hands to his sight and saw the teeth of ignorance were tightly dug in. He could not use his hands to free himself; his mind convinced him it would be useless to try. It was at this point, more miraculous still that the man began to cry.

Someone in the distance, far in front, heard the man's whimper and came back to try to help. Seeing this man sitting in the road, crying in pain and agony caused the stranger to look for a way to sooth this poor creature. Then the stranger saw the problem and said he'd been down this road before and knew just what to do.

One by one, the stranger took those teeth out of the man's hands. The man at first jumped with the anticipation of greater pain, now numbed by shock watched as the stranger used his hands with amazing skill, and finally retracted all the teeth.

The man tried to thank the stranger but instead the stranger offered some advice. Before leaving the stranger cautioned the man about reaching out in blindness with his hands, and that he would have to look after his hands with more care.

Our man stood up, walked to his home, and carefully looked at his hands. They still tingled, for the bites were vicious, but the intense pain had gone away. The man stretched out his hands as if for the very first time. He was amazed by what they had gone through, but now he understood.

His hands, like yours, are gifts you see, that not everyone, unfortunately has. Some of us are born with stumps, some are born with mutations, but we learn that whatever we have it is better than having nothing. It is hard to create a thought or image in your mind that always fits, but our hands give us the power to make things real, and that includes the abstract.

The man finally knew his hands were there, of which there was no doubt from the beginning. But now he knew just what they're for. His hands now had meaning.

The Dance of the Man

It was the night of a party at the home of the man. The room where most of the guests congregated was full of life. Many of these people sat around, talking with those they knew and some they didn't. It was supposed to be a party, but it was strange for there was no music to be heard, only the droning sound from the different conversations.

On one side of the room the man sat alone, hands to his face. He was very quiet and he bothered to speak to no one. He hardly even seemed to breathe. The only sign of life he possessed was the shaking in one of his feet, just a slight twitch from his ankle down. No one paid attention to the man or his foot, which moved to a rhythm understood only by his semi-unconscious mind.

After a short time, the twitch of his foot was accompanied by a slow manipulation of his fingers. Everyone else in the room was still minding their own business, not knowing the meaning of the man's movements. It did become apparent to them that the man was alive and moving, however they knew they too were alive, and had their own problems. The man was still quiet, but he continued the minute movements of his fingers and foot.

Time passed and the man began to flex his arms and legs; first this way, then another. They too were not movements that caused alarm to those who saw them. Everyone still in their own circle; doing what they did before; minded their own business and talked.

One person who sat in another corner of the room had observed the man since his movements began. Slightly concerned of what she saw, she left her seat to take one at the man's side. For a moment, he stopped moving. She leaned over and whispered in his ear "is everything alright?" He only nodded; a signal she took as an affirmative. She quietly got up and returned to her seat in the corner. When she sat down, the man slowly began his movements again, all from the seat of his chair.

The man soon removed his hands from his face and rose from his seat. For a brief moment, everyone looked at him, but then flashed their attention back to what they had been doing. It was at that moment that the man started to dance.

It was a funny kind of dance being there was no music in the air or anywhere else one could attest to. It was a slow dance. It included the twitch of his foot, the slow manipulation of his fingers and hands, and the flexing of his arms and legs. As soon as one movement was noticed, another started. It was slow, very slow, but the man's total being was in motion.

The room became quiet as everyone focused their attention to the man who danced without music. The sound of a hand clap and finger snaps came from the corner where his first observer sat. It was all quite spontaneous and took everyone by surprise. It was followed by other finger snaps and hand claps, each becoming louder and more frequent. These sounds affected the dancing man in a unique way, his movements became faster.

The room's attention was now split between the sounds of the snaps and claps, and the sight of the dancing man. One by one, the people followed the example of the one in the corner, clapping their hands and snapping their fingers. The man now intrigued by the increased sound in the room began stomping his foot to the floor. It was quickly copied by the one in the corner, and gradually by everyone in the room. No one noticed there was no music.

From deep inside the belly of the man came a moan and a groan. The sound within him mixed with the sound of the room, which was itself beginning to multiply as more people participated in the goings on.

The more the sound in the room grew, the faster the man danced. He now jumped up and down, his body gyrating in many directions and with no apparent pattern. The sounds vibrated everything, and the vibrations became more sounds, all which made the man dance with more vigor to the music in his mind.

The movements of the dance and the sound in the room became a kind of heat. Everyone sweated. The dance was now feverish. And the observer from the corner joined the man on the floor. The others followed suit, as everyone was out of their seat dancing in the middle of the floor.

As the dance went on, the sound and heat in the room increased. The heat produced a kind of glow in the form of light. The dancing man saw the light and felt the heat seemingly for the first time. Looking around suddenly, he saw everyone dancing to the rhythms of his mind. Then just as suddenly as he started, he stopped dancing and fell silent to his seat. When this happened, the light, heat, and the sounds in the room stopped.

Everyone noticed the difference in the room and looked towards the man now slumped over in his chair. The observer said to the now sensitive crowd, "The man is dead".

(He was the life of the party.)

Reality

"Hello?"… "Who is there?"…

I asked those questions when I first awoke the night I experienced that horrible dream. I stared off into the darkness towards something I sensed there. But I saw nothing.

Three times in the past, I envisioned such a dream, one that scared the living daylights out of me. In the first one, I saw myself surrounded by many faces, people familiar to my childhood. It seems they all wore alarming expressions on their faces, and they seemed to be trying to transmit their feelings verbally… at least their mouths were moving and their tongues were lagging. But I heard nothing.

Then the scene changed, with my essence now outside that ring of faces. I now saw them as a backdrop to the asphalt playground that witnessed my growth from youth through adolescence. White and yellow lines marked out the same base paths and courts at the real playground of my childhood's memory. However, this was just a dream…

The steel mesh fence surrounding the playground showed the same damage the real one suffered. As I looked outward further, I saw my youngest brother stumble through one hole in the fence then fall to the ground. More figures swarmed around the area where he fell, and soon, my presence joined an ever-quickening pace. Suddenly, everything went black. The next image my mind created showed me carrying my brother to the place we both called home. At this point, I wake up, shake my head, then return to sleep.

When I become scared, I feel my heartbeat clear up to my temples. Normally, I sense my heartbeat there as a gentle throbbing only. When I'm afraid, it seems as if there is a little man standing in mid air just off my brow, kicking me in the head with his combat boots. Accompanying the harsh feeling of my heartbeat at the temples, is a kind of swelling pressure inside my chest. It is as if that same little man has a twin in my chest who practices his bad habit of blowing up balloons to their capacity, whenever he knows I'm afraid.

Yeah, I know when I'm afraid, and this dream scared me before a single image flashed in my mind. When I closed my eyes in sleep, I heard a thumping in the distance...coming ever closer. I attempted to move, but in that dream, my presence remained frozen to the spot. I could not even turn my head. It was as if I was dead. There was nothing but darkness around me. I couldn't see. I couldn't feel. I only heard that thumping coming closer, but ever so slowly.

I panicked, and felt my heart beating where it shouldn't be. The sound came closer and got louder. I struggled against the invisible bonds holding me, and upon failing, I became scared. My heartbeat was now more pronounced at my temples and neck, as my heart seemed to want to explode out of my chest. It was beating that hard. I looked out again and still saw only darkness, yet the thumping sound was very close now. I should have been able to see it, but I didn't.

Reaching out, my hand fell upon an object at my side… a flashlight… and with it in hand I tried once more to break the bonds that held me immobile. With all the strength in my body, I pulled against the bonds and simultaneously flicked on the flashlight only to find myself sitting up in bed, awake, and staring off into the darkness of my room.

The only evidence remaining from the experience convincing me to this very day that something existed nearby was the wild rapid thumping in my chest. A hazy mist seemed to disappear underneath the crack of the closed door as I hit the light, and those words I heard fall from my lips seemingly spontaneously with my awakening. "Hello! Who is there?"

3:30 AM April 11, 2004

I know not what to call this yet, but what happened to me was all in a dream, one that was so real that I woke up at 3:30 in the morning, calling out for help, and fearing for my life. Please read what follows, and maybe you may enlighten me on just what I did wrong.

First I have to say I pride myself on not having made any enemies for myself, with either my actions or words all throughout my life. I know no one who hates me, nor do I know anyone I have given a reason to do so, not even my ex-wife. But in my dream I met such a man who hated me enough to make an attempt on my life. And the worse thing about it, I do not know how the dream ends, for I awoke before the issues were resolved.

Let me start at the beginning. I was dressed for a black tie affair, and with a woman for whom I had hopes but no history. Her skin color matched my own and the medium black dress she wore did nothing to hide the curves it covered. Her hair sat mostly on top of her head, with a short row of bangs, with a few thick, well-maintained strands flowing down the nape of her neck above her shoulders. Her voice sang in the low alto range, thick, heavy and sensual. I got the impression I liked her and I felt very comfortable to be with her but I do not even remember her name. She was driving so it must have been her car.

We rode uneventfully together to somewhere I got the impression was my first time going, and that she was showing me the way. The road to the place of the affair hugged around a very large hill or mount, up above yet still within a city. As we arrived at the venue, I knew it to be a large resort type hotel, very ritzy, secluded, and very tall. Valets took the car as we drove to the door, and we entered the glass doors together, smiling, and holding hands. I felt happy.

We walked to a set of escalators that rose to a mezzanine level terrace. The terrace afforded a magnificent view of the city, distinguishable by multi-colored lights that outlined roads running for miles in all directions, and of buildings that filled in the dark spaces between the streets. I was amazed by the atmosphere.

I remember then we rode a small well-lit stewarded elevator to the tenth floor, and went to what must have been her room, to door that read 1035. I got the impression we did not stay there long but left soon to the seventh floor where there was a large bar, a combo playing in the background, and several pool tables. The lady sat down at the bar, and was served by a bartender she seemed to know. I became a spectator for what seemed to happen next.

The bartender, a Caucasian man of about my height and medium build, stone cold blue eyes and short straight brown hair wore a black vest and bow tie long sleeved white shirt and black pants that appeared to be the uniform of employ. He came from behind the bar and set up a pool table for the game 9-ball that was to be played with my date. What I saw then were the three most remarkable games I ever witnessed.

On his first shot, the bartender knocked in the ball he was supposed to, as the cue ball then slammed into the nine after bouncing off the rail, and the nine rolled slowly into a side pocket...end of game. On his second shot, the first of the second game, he again sank the nine ball off the break. My date broke after the set up for the third game and left a series of balls along the rail. The bartender with one shot sank all the balls along that rail into the corner pocket by which I stood, and the last one to fall was the nine.

I could not believe my eyes, and I could not contain my excitement. I spoke to the bartender, complimenting him on the most remarkable shooting I had ever seen. He looked at me with anger in his eyes, for what I did not understand.

He became belligerent in a most subtle kind of way, by acting as if I were not even present. I said again that I very much enjoyed watching the way he played, and he walked up to me and pushed me. I was really confused then.

Wanting not to cause a problem, I walked away from the table, but he followed and pushed me again, with both of his hands to my chest. I turned to look for the lady I escorted and she was not there. I stopped at the entrance to the bar pool room on my way out, and motioned to the bartender and he came to my beckon. I apologized for any misunderstanding between us, and offered my hand for a shake. He appeared to accept the handshake, but when I said I had only sought to compliment him, he again antagonistically pushed me out of the room. I heard myself say "this is shit, and I am going to make a complaint."

I remember getting into the elevator but seeing I could only go as low as the fourth floor. As I reached for the button for the lowest floor, a steward took my hand and squeezed it hard, while looking at me with anger and hatred in his heart. Somehow, the elevated descended to the lobby.

I looked for and found a desk manned by several uniformed ladies. I asked, "What should I do to make a complaint about two members of the staff?" I was first asked about the nature of the complaint, and then given a paperback book shaped document to be completed.

As I began working on the document, from the corner of my eye, I saw as both the bartender and the steward walked past me into an employee office or locker room. They exited the hotel with their coats and hats before I did.

The more I looked into the document, the more confused I got. Each page seemed to lead me to a point, then offer no way for me to explain my experiences of which I sought to complain. I felt so frustrated by trying to fill out the document that I yelled. I told the people behind the desk that this is form is not helping me, that it was frustrating, then threw it down on the counter, and exited the building.

The confusion I felt now went beyond what I experienced in the hotel, as I walked into what I thought was the direction of the road only to find myself approaching a very high narrow ledge. Being deathly afraid of heights, I turned around and went the other way. I still did not know where I was, but found the road that lead to the hotel. At first I walked down the road, but soon began a jog down the hill.

I was starting to feel comfortable with my pace, when up ahead about a hundred fifty to two hundred feet away, moving in my direction and pointing a handgun at me was the bartender. He shot a few times before I even realized it was happening. As I turned around and tried to run back up the hill, I felt afraid that my life would end at the hand of some person I do not know, for something I do not understand. And this in the dream is where I found myself yelling the word, "help!"

This is when and where I woke up. I heard myself whimpering in the darkness of my living room, feeling helpless and afraid, while curled up in a ball on the couch where I had fallen asleep. And this is when I started thinking about all the confusion and anxieties I feel when I try to complete my application for certification. I thought of how confusing and overwhelming the process is to provide information of my past that must come from other people. It's like going to ask someone who is dead to me about the work I have done in my life. And because the completion of the application is so important to my continued ability to work professionally, I began to feel afraid of the possible expulsion from a field of endeavor I love and according to some, am very competent in.

I guess that is why I dream of a situation that ends with my having fear for my life at the hands of a stranger.

Help!

The States of Mind

I once went on a journey through the country of my mind, in a 12 wheeled chariot guided by a silver dog insignia on its forward armored plate. A long and treacherous trip it was for the roadway of my mind passed through several states... from the hell I was in, to the safety of the peace I desired and would find, if only I could be acquitted at the trial of my decisions along the road.

The first state was an Arid Zone; a pure hell. Dry and barren of all life, my Arid Zone had but one contribution. It brought fear into my heart, for who wants to die in hell. I saw those that did in the form of lifeless trees that lined the roadway with branches that reached up high as if begging for another chance to live. I had my chance so I left this state.

From hell, I came to the State of New Magic... that land of enchantment. Darkness abounded, there was nothing to see. I knew I could stay there forever; it could be my destiny unless I came down off my cloud and realized my wrongs. I did not leave my chariot in that state of mystical thinking, but purged my soul with black coffee. Then I slowly descended from that state of mystical enchantment.

"Everybody Must Pay Their Dues" read the sign as I passed into the State of Taxes. I was paying mine before the journey started. When I came to the State of Taxes, I knew the worst was yet to come. It was there where I spent my morning; I knew Oz came after noon. I also knew once I got through that, nightfall would bring Misery.

In Oz the sun was shining bright; there was no green on the trees. My mind here went in circles for an unbelievably long time and everything stayed the same. In Oz, I could not take the pressure, because the road was clearer now. I saw it all the way to my destination, and through every state I would go. I thought of running, of ending it all, but knew the Arid Zone would await me. My form would be a lifeless tree. So humbly I left the state of Oz to enter at nightfall the state of Misery.

On the far side of this state lay the City of Saints, along the River Styx. I had to make it there. The sounds of death surrounded the darkened chariot and struck my heart with fear. Along the road, the trees bent towards me; there touch being the death I feared. I squirmed, I moaned, and my feeble attempts to escape it made my misery no easier to take, but I took it, and at the first gleam of the morning light, my salvation in the City of Saints could be seen on the horizon. The roughest part of my journey was over.

Within the city I made the decision to continue my trip. I prepared myself for the states yet to come. I tossed away my clothing worn in the land of the dead for across the River Styx lay the land of the living. No longer was the fear of death at hand, but the realization of life's problems took its place. In my pocket, I kept a pipe through which dreams could be found. No longer wanting to dream, the pipe and the dreams it contained were discarded along with the dead land clothing. Then, my journey continued.

I crossed the River Styx into a State of Illness. My resistance was not yet strong, but I weathered the storm.

More coffee purged my soul, soup helped break a little fever, and sleep cured my restlessness, as I continued through Illness and the physical State of Indigestion.

Another high caused me to awake. My head was spinning and I felt confused about it because I had taken no drugs. Maybe this high was a relapse, but no, just another state of mind. This state was amazingly long, but not very good. Drugs gave me a better high, but this was natural euphoria. There was no fear of the police dragging me off and locking me up forever, for in this state, everybody brags of the high they have.

I lay back again, rested, and passed into the State of Pain. This pain was not as physical as were the states of Illness and Indigestion. This pain took the form of fear; the fear of making the wrong decision for my trip was almost over. There were things needing to be done, with the wrong things meaning banishment back to the Arid Zone State. Only a New Jury for my trial could tell whether my decisions were right or wrong. But before entering the court, I had to wait my turn in the City of Humanitarian Devotion on the border of the State of Pain.

I reached my destination, the State of the New Jury, where the judgment was to me revealed. The trial lasted two weeks. Friends and relatives testified; some for and some against my case. Evidence came from every state through which I passed to get to the trial. Most of the testimonials were in my favor until the judge received the report of my actions in the Arid Zone State.

Only there did I fail, and only there should I return to right my wrongs and bring a new hope to the lifeless souls there. To the Arid Zone State I went again, passing over the other states I had passed through getting to my trial. The jury was tough, the next time they will be tougher, but the judge was the toughest of all, for no one can ever be tougher on me than a judge which is myself.

The States of Mind (Poem)

Arizona is the Arid Zone
Yes it's hot as Hell
New Mexico is New Magic
If I stayed there I would yell
Texas is for Taxes
Everyone must pay their dues
Oklahoma was the State of Oz
Everyone there sings the blues
Missouri sounds like misery
Illinois is like illness too
Indiana gave me indigestion
(and some heartburn ooooh)
Ohio is that new high
You heard me speaking of
from Pennsylvania you'll find pain
Philadelphia does mean love
But New Jersey is my home state
It's where my jury lives
It's where I'll find my true love
It is where nothing rhymes

A Ring for the Collection

Once upon a time in the land of eternal sunshine, perched between the mountains, along the banks of the mighty Desert River was the shimmering city of the great firebird.

In that city lived a beautiful brown eyed princess who was named after the homeland of Virginia. Her father was a royal chieftain prince, and her mother, God rest her soul, was the Madonna of the family tribe.

Virginia was a special princess, known far and wide that she loved and cared for her father as he grew older. Every single day after performing her own royal duties, she hurried to his side and catered to the needs of his castle. She often let him oversee important ceremonial duties in and around her own palace, though she was more than capable of doing them herself, just to help make him feel needed and appreciated.

Everyone also knew Virginia to be very friendly and helpful to people that often came to visit her land. She was so nice, as she walked by, broken hearts became mended, and lost souls became found.

Virginia was nice to know and fun to be with.

Virginia loved her royal robes of purple, or lavender, and maroon, but especially the one of black and red. She loved to see the classic actresses perform over and over in stories of delight or in those with a scary thrill.

She loved the music made by the innovative mathematical wizards of instrumental sound, and to move to its melodic and rhythmic incantations.

Virginia loved to spend time in her garden when she took time to herself. She grew flowers and fruits and cactus, built walkways, and weeded it all by hand. Of all the things she loved though, Virginia loved her father best. And after him, was her collection of rings.

The rings Virginia collected were filled with special powers and charms. One ring carried within its stone the love of its giver, and when she wore it, the love inside would free the hearts of the people she passed in her travels.

One ring's band of gold filled the pantries of the poor with the tastiest and most nutritious tidbits whenever she wore it while in their company. All the rings Virginia's collection did something nice like that for all the people she came into contact with, or those she passed as she traveled along the road.

The only person the rings could do nothing for was Virginia, as she was forbidden to use their power for herself. And Virginia was very happy with that arrangement.

But one day, as fate would have it, Virginia was put under the spell of an evil sorcerer. He wanted to control the power within the collection of the magical rings. He tried to steal them, but the rings would not leave the safety of Virginia's palace. So instead of stealing them, he kidnapped Virginia. He kept her from her father, and her royal duties.

He hid her from the people she passed by every day in her travels. He was that mean.

Everyone felt miserable but they did not notice that Virginia was being held captive against her will by the sorcerer. Virginia's father, the royal prince became very depressed because Virginia was not there to help him. He fell into a deep sleep that looked so much like death, except for the tears that occasionally fell from his closed eyes, and the sound of him crying heard throughout the city.

The evil sorcerer was very mean to Virginia. He was so mean, the sun hid itself from the land of eternal sunshine, the warmth of the shimmering city turned ice cold...and it rained all the time.

And so, the evil sorcerer said to everyone, "I will bring the sunshine back, I will make the warmth return, and I will make the rain clouds disappear. But for me to do that, I must have a magic ring too." He was telling a great big fib.

All of the people were horrified and frightened because of the change in the weather. They knew the sorcerer was so mean that if they gave him a magic ring he would use it for no good. They did not know what to do. So a call went out far and wide for help.

It was this call for help that attracted the attention of a very sensitive prince who lived in a fertile land by the sea, perched between the city of humanitarian devotion and the city of the big apple.

The prince made his fame by removing pain from the people who suffered. It was, perhaps, the sound of suffering that made him load his possessions onto his old trusted bull, Taurus, and leave for the valley of the shimmering city.

It took the prince an arduous three day journey to arrive finally at the once shimmering city. After arriving there, he began to remove the fears of the people just by listening to their cries. The prince then sought out all the knowledge he could, that could help him understand what had gone wrong in such a beautiful place.

The prince began to peer into a super window of knowledge, and pushed down mystic alphabet buttons in a secret order. It was through the window that the prince saw what had gone wrong with the city surrounded the disappearance of the princess Virginia, and the false promises of the evil sorcerer.

The prince went to Virginia's palace looking for a way to remove her from the spell of the evil sorcerer. It was there that he heard the weeping sounds of the magical collection of rings.

One of the rings from Virginia's collection, the one with the singing story stone, sang of how the sorcerer coveted their power, and kidnapped Virginia. It also told the prince that with all their magic power, the rings were unable to help when it came to Virginia.

The prince went back to the supernatural window of knowledge, and asked it how he could make a magical ring that could save Virginia.

The window replied "The ring to save her must only work for her safety. The sorcerer must not want it, or be able to use it. The only way that could happen is if you give up a piece of your heart, and place it in the ring. Only then will you be able to save her."

The prince pulled away from the window, feeling a tingling sensation of fear. He had once before tried to rescue a princess with his heart, but she turned out to be the princess of the witches' coven, and he almost died from the pain she gave him. But the prince knew that unless he acted to save Virginia, the whole city would suffer from the ranting and ravings of the evil sorcerer.

So the prince went to the local alchemist and ordered a special ring. The ring's jewel was a black onyx stone heart-shaped to hold a part of the prince's heart. It was held in place with a setting of strong looking arms. Its band was made of silver, yellow gold and white gold. It was all bonded together with a drop of the prince's blood.

The prince then took the ring to the evil sorcerer. And the prince, while pretending to be a friend to the evil warlock said to him "This is the magic ring you wanted. It has great power so be very careful when you wear it."

The evil sorcerer snatched the ring, and tried to put it on but it was too small for his fingers. The prince then said in a coy manner, "try it on the lady over there" pointing towards Virginia, "to get an idea of how it works.

Knowing her magic rings would not work to help her, the evil sorcerer slipped it on her middle finger. Virginia woke up. Thunder and lightning were heard immediately, and the rain stopped. The sun came out and the warmth returned.

As Virginia rose to her feet, the sorcerer tried to place her back under his spell, but his evil incantations just bounced off her. He tried to grab her, but the prince jumped in his way. And Virginia was then able to walk out of the life of the evil sorcerer, forever.

When the people saw Virginia, they became happy again. When she went to the castle of her father, he awoke from his near death-like sleep. And the prince who saved her, became welcome in all of Virginia's duties and delights.

And they lived happily ever after.

Part of the Miracle

Do you know what a miracle is? It is something to marvel over...something wonderful, and beyond the ordinary. It is a gift, a gift from God. Many people know that when Jesus walked the Earth, he performed the kind of miracles only God could. But did you know God gave us the power to perform miracles, without giving us the knowledge we were performing them. Very few of us even have the ability to see we performed our miraculous works even years after the fact. Let me give you an example.

We all have seen pictures of people starving for food, lacking in shelter from storms, victims of wars, and the horrible atrocities man places on other men. Every close-up of the children shows eyes that reflect no light and no glimmer of hope appears in those large, deep orbs.

Those same eyes scan the horizons and see only clouds way out there. They offer a prayer to God for the hope those clouds will bring a much needed rain, to nourish their crops, and fill their wells. Maybe, they hope momentarily, a bountiful harvest results from that darkness rising at the edge of the Earth. Instead, a huge ravenous flock of birds devour the valuable freshly planted seeds.

Or maybe pestilence, storms, infestations, floods or quakes schemed either alone or in concert to wreck havoc in the lives of those innocent victims.

Those same big dark eyes search the horizon when another cloud appears way out there. They offer another prayer to

God. Maybe they hope momentarily, if they plant seeds again, this cloud will bring rain. Maybe the crops will grow. Maybe the harvest insures the presence of plentiful food this winter and next year! They plant the scarce seeds as the cloud gets closer. But it is not rain. It is dust from trucks driven by soldiers who come to kill their parents, to burn their village, and leave those sad eyed children homeless, scared, without proper guidance, and consumed by hatred.

Or maybe poverty, addiction, human slavery, lack of education, and non caring bureaucracy schemed, either alone or in concert to deprive their victims of human dignity, and contribute to the perpetuation of their evils.

Whatever the culprit, the results are the same. The victims lose hope and self esteem. They hate. Anger dominates their interactions with others. They become victimizers. And they blame it all on what happened or failed to happen at just the right time in their lives.

So now when they look towards the horizon and another cloud materializes way out there, their eyes too weak to open wide, and they themselves so malnourished they can shed no tears. There are no more seeds to plant or seeds of hope. There is no more food to eat or spiritual nourishment. They are too tired or weak to offer to God the prayer that is in their hearts. And they are having a very hard time believing at that point that a good God even exists, especially since as the clouds get closer they see trucks that look like the ones that brought the soldiers.

Hatred and self pity fills their heart, while anger and resentment for all others form without a thought.

This is where our miracle occurs. This time, the trucks bring food, medicine, tools, seeds, books, cloth, clothing, and blankets. Now they eat, heal, work the fields, work their mind, stay warm, nourish their bodies and minds, and get strong again. And they fall to their knees to give thanks, expressing gratitude to the God that heard their silent cries.

How wonderful is God that He saves many lives on our planet daily by this kind of intercession. Yes, God hears the cries and the weak bodied prayers of children, the ill, and the homeless. Yes, God insures the delivery of the needed supplies in every quarter. Yet, it was our hearts, softened by the images of those works of evil that prompted our giving that made the miracle possible.

But now we turn a deaf ear to the sound of the suffering and the needy. It overwhelms our senses to see the homeless, to smell the stench of poverty and mental imbalance. We've become too selfish to be a part of the miracle God designed us to be. Each of us is a link in God's chain that is only as strong as our weakest member. Our end will come sooner and more dramatically if our chain is too weak.

Give freely from your hearts your time to whatever charity softens your heart to produce other miracles to serve the greater good. Be a part of the next miracles in the eyes of those in need.

The Story of Life

The sun shined as brightly that day as it had every day since we last saw any sight of land. In a four-man out-rigger canoe, my companions and I knew but one thing … stroke. I remember all those thoughts I had, but never spoke them. The water of the sea embodied our entire reality. The only land that might exist was where the mountain range known as the Andes used to be. War destroyed all else.

My three companions and I were the only survivors of a war in which the weapons used could not be controlled nor could their unimaginable destructive power. All that remained from man's great technologies was the canoe and paddles we used to direct us to where we rumored amongst ourselves we would find land.

The journey taxed our mental stamina and physical strength. The sun never set. It just sat there, stationary in the center of the sky. We doubted we were moving any closer to our goal, but we stroked just the same.

And those thoughts I thought before came to me, but again never spoke them. They made sense. Why not just stop and die here, for is that not the inevitable conclusion of our escapade? We prolong the agony just by going on, I'd reason. We work ourselves to a frazzle but continue to stroke. At every stroke came that same thought. The same question stabbed in the back of my mind. Why not just stop and die? I heard only one response to this silent question, and that was the sound of the splash made the next time the paddles hit the water.

85

Time passed. Eternity it seems could have ended and been reborn countless splashes prior when we saw a rock in the distance jutting out of the waters. Its shape looked like a tower isolated on a desolate plateau.

We directed our craft towards it and disembarked on our arrival, only to witness our craft sink into the sea of oblivion. This left us no recourse but to climb this rock. It appeared to be no more than fifty feet above or heads. We climbed straight up the steep incline. We told ourselves that if we'd throw an arm over the top, and we'd be able to hold on at the summit forever. But that thought returned to me. Why not just stop and die? This time no splash sounded. No answer came and the questions remained.

We made our way to the top, threw an arm over the top and began to pull ourselves up when suddenly, the sun moved. Then the rock, itself moved, constantly changing shape and increasing in size. We held on; no longer trying to pull ourselves over; just holding on.

And that thought came back. Why not just let go? Why not just give in? To end this agony would be a blessing. Why prolong it? The more the mountain moved the faster the thoughts came. I looked down to find the ocean of eternity was gone from sight and our feet dangled high above nothingness. Would it be an eternal drop with death at its bottom? Those questions came again. Why must I hold on? Why? And still, there was no answer.

Eternity passed. My companions and I were still holding on when suddenly, everything stopped. The mountain ceased its metamorphic and phenomenal growth. The sun suspended its chaotic orbit. The unspoken questions disappeared along with the thoughts that nurtured them. Together we pulled ourselves over the top to witness unfolding before our eyes a garden supreme as beautiful as the fabled Eden.

Then I knew why I held on at the mountain. I knew the reason I continued to stroke on the ocean, although I questioned my soul. And the answers to all my doubts came as the silent questions themselves fell from my lips. I hoped good fruit grew from my struggles. It's because life is worth having over eternal slumber.

The Coming of the Third World

There was once a day when everyone had forgotten they lived in the second world and that the first had been destroyed by water. Everyone looks forward to such perfect weather conditions. No complaints surfaced. Just enough temperature and humidity made it very comfortable outside. A slight breeze blew gently. Small and puffy clouds looked like of creatures alive long ago.

This day, however, something else about the sky caused suspicion and fear. A fiery, bright orange hue illuminated the sky, the envelope of the earth. Clouds appeared pink in sharp contrast. Grey colored trees and grass cast eerie purplish tinted shadows. The seas reflected a murky brown. And the sun which no one could understand for it rose in the north, was green… a very dark green.

No one knew what the strange colors meant. The leaders of the world refused to panic. They knew to blame the work of their enemies for the unnerving celestial events. Governments set up investigating committees as if they previously planned for such a day. Generals alerted their militaries, to defend against a surprise attack. But the day felt beautiful, except for that nobody recognized the beauty of the colors.

Scientists called conferences to explain the colors, a feat they truthfully could not accomplish, but they tried anyway. They contrived statistics measuring how the colors affected crime, sex, and mortality for the eyes of the people. They conjured up fact after fact about creation of the colors.

Then they brought the results of their experiments to the knowledge of the leaders.

The sun reached the center point of the sky when reason and common sense tried to infiltrate the minds of the leaders and scientists alike. Cries from the populace told the leaders to stop their folly and accept the color. Students and teachers banded together to empower their association with the colors. Socialists and capitalists debated each other for the dominant view of the colors. The officials refused to listen. All this occurred because no one understood the truth behind the colors.

After the noon, the colors kept changing and the leaders began to act. They commanded the militaries and aimed the missiles. Soldiers and airmen followed their orders blindly and armed themselves, and the sailors went to battle stations. They prepared for war, without knowing which enemy to fight. The evening rapidly approached.

The sun hovered near the southern horizon when a black cloud appeared in the middle of the sky. It encompassed everything. The leaders panicked and pushed their buttons. The missiles went up, but they failed come down. The sky erupted in fire. The leaders heard screams of the masses for the first time. Nothing worked. Then they all realized the inevitable.

Everyone rushed to repent. They packed placed of worship beyond their capacity. The fire in the sky came closer to the earth. The prayers increased in their intensity and volume.

Everywhere it was the same… Peoples interacted with one another in ways thought impossible by previous minds.

Then a voice… a singular voice of choral range and intensity sang out to every ear. It spoke in a universal language understood by all. It told about the colors, the world, and its own nature. It told of the many chances man missed to change the outcome of that day. Nobody moved, everyone listened, and the fireball touched the earth.

The darkness lifted, birthing a new dawn, and the colors mattered not. The people played and enjoyed the day. Music filled the air everywhere. It was the coming of the third world.

My Journey Section

Only if you care to know
on this journey I had to go
and at its end my discovery
was the person that is me

The Gift

God made me different. I was born cross-eyed, and for many years, I hated when people reminded of it. For most of my childhood other kids teased with almost every name relating to eyes they thought of, like cock-eyed, Cyclops, hawk-eye, four eyed, etc. I got into fights when they pointed out the characteristic that set me apart from the rest them. I even tried corrective surgery, but it failed to clear up my minor imperfection, and bring the inner peace for which I so desperately searched.

I thought God hated me and sought to punish me by giving me these eyes. I lacked acceptance of the reality. The more the truth about my eyes was told to me, the more I fought. I lost more fights than most kids in the neighborhood had. I needed something to happen or the direction I headed in was wrought with peril.

The turning point came when I began to look at my crossed eyes as a blessing instead of a curse. I asked myself, "Why would God give me these crossed eyes. Surely there must be a good reason." Then I realized my eyes gave me clear, distinct vision in two directions at the same time. I rationalized God's gift allowed me to view any situation or problem from two points of view at the same time. Since coming to that conclusion, I have never gotten into another fight because of how my eyes were different from everyone else.

What gift stands you apart from mostly everyone? Why do you consider it a curse? How can you view it as a blessing?

My Relationship with My Mother

Last night I began thinking about my relationship with my mother. Somehow, now it seems that I did not bond to her in the same manner of my brothers and sisters. I was never able to confide in her from the earliest time in my life that I remember, and for a long time I was so angry at her I even said I hated her. Since she was always supportive to my positive efforts and never laid a hand on me for my negative ones, I think the reason for not bonding with her had to be something unknown to me from before I was three.

During my teenage years, after my father moved in with her girlfriend, my mother began to drink. When she was drunk she began to accuse me of things, and told me I would be just like my father. I was angry at her for that, and when I graduated high school, I could not wait to leave the home, and that is why I went into the Navy. On my way to the check in, my father drove, and my mother came along, and she cried the entire time just because I was leaving.

It took me a few years to get past my anger, but still never really felt close to her. She would send me things I knew she could not afford to when I came out to ASU in the 70's, and gave me a roof over my head when I went back to Jersey. I could not wait to get my first job and moved out as soon as I could. I could not find it in me to call her just because. In a lot of ways, I was just selfish in my relationship with her and others.

My mother died years ago, and once I got past my lack of a personal bond, I was able to look at her with a different set of eyes. She was a remarkable woman, who welcomed my friends, tried to send me off in the right direction in my life, was very supportive, and provided me with a passive kind of guidance. I don't know that if she was still alive that I would have improved my bond with her the way it has improved in her death.

Home Coming 1985

Having received the funds from friends made in another world, it is time to make a trip home. Personal items had to be left, since this is meant only to be a short visit, Mother has cancer. Air travel is the quickest way, the chosen way. No one knows I'm coming.

Things have changed since the old days. Only six of the sixteen buildings are occupied. New dangers lurk everywhere. People look at me as if I'm new to this place, but the old-timers they remember. New friends of the family wonder who I am. I'm a stranger in my own home.

The news of Mother's cancer was known, but the new dangers were striking down other members of the family. C-cane, Girl, Crack - call it what you will. It had my baby sister and two brothers going wild, and it chased and caught hold of me, too. We were no longer fiscally responsible; rent fell behind, and there was no food in the house.

Mother comes first. There are some people that are not compared to anyone, and no one is or can be compared to them. Mother is one of those, a rare breed, who lived up to the highest moral principles. Only an occasional drink prevents her nomination for sainthood.

In the day when women strive for self effacing fulfillments and pleasure, Mother lives just for her children and grandchildren. Even after Daddy left the house to live with her best friend turned fiend, she never asked for much.

She never had other men in the house or outside of it. Her life was her family. Though it would have been simple for her to go onto welfare she never did. If daddy did not give of the children did not give, she went without. She made all our friends welcome in our home.

My Langston Heritage
(Most Updated version)

An obsession existed within me since childhood. It caused me to wonder about who I was, and where I came from. My name is George Langston Cook. My father's first name was also George, but he told me he really disliked the idea of having a son named Junior, so my mother named me after her uncle, George instead. Therefore, my name came from someone I never met or knew anything about. My mother gave me her maiden name "Langston" as my middle name, which is an old Sothern tradition. I grew up wondering about her side of the family, but kept that curiosity to myself. I felt isolated from that family.

My mother, Lucy Mae Langston had an interesting background, considering the time and place she grew up. She was born in rural, segregated North Carolina in 1921. My aunt Mary, my mother's oldest sister raised her in Norfolk, Virginia after their mother died when my mother was six years old. She graduated from a Catholic high school where her curriculum was academic instead of vocational. She worked in a Norfolk hospital for 3 years as a Nurse's Aide. After the outbreak of World War II, my mother entered the Army Air Corps and served as a medical corpsman in what appears to have been a segregated unit. She reached the rank of corporal before her discharge at the war's end. Those activities alone made her an uncommon Black woman for those times.

During her military service, my mother met my father George Henry Cook (who is another story for another time). They were stationed together on the base at Walla Walla, Washington. They exchanged wedding vows there on August 6, 1945. Upon their discharge from the military, they moved to my father's adopted home in Newark, New Jersey.

My mother told me stories about being part of a large family she lost contact with. Her mother, Mary "Maggie" Hoskins, died when she was six and her father Hugh "Tobe" Langston died the year I was born. I never saw their pictures, or heard stories about them. I knew my mother had a sister, some brothers and a half sister. She mentioned her oldest brother may have become a doctor and lived around Boston. She said one of my ancestors served in Congress. I even remember that we visited a farm belonging to her relatives somewhere down South when I was very young, too.

Only a couple of her relatives made their presence known to us on a regular basis while I was growing up. There was my Aunt Mary, my mother's oldest sister, who sent us the fruitcake every Christmas. We would visit her and her husband Selton in Norfolk every few years. And then there was Liz my aunt Mary's only child, who lived in Philadelphia and visited us from time to time along with her son Tony, and husband Jimmy. Jimmy and Liz drank a whole lot, and always ended up arguing or fighting before they went home. And that was it for the Langston side of the family, so I thought.

I completed high school in 1970, and entered the Navy. After about eight months, I was sent to a training base around the Norfolk area, where my Aunt Mary and Uncle Selton still lived. They always welcomed me, and I visited them often. I found their home to be a pleasant respite from my military life. I could have a bedroom with a large soft comfortable bed all to myself instead of the crowed berthing areas with their hard thin mattresses. It was always so peaceful and quiet there, and also very dull.

I expected a faster pace than in their style of living. No young adults or anyone else near my age group lived in that home, only my aunt and uncle. I remember one day I met one of my mother's childhood girlfriends there. That may have been the highlight of visiting there. Then one day, my Aunt Mary took me to the home of my uncle, William Hugh Langston who also lived in Norfolk. He and his wife Dot welcomed me with open arms.

William Hugh Langston was my mother's youngest full blooded brother, but I remember hearing nothing about him before visiting him. To my knowledge, he and his family never came to Newark, and I really don't recall ever visiting his home either. Yet, he had many pictures of my sibling and I in his photo albums, including my recent high school graduation and Navy recruit pictures.

Music, drinking, smoking, and card playing activity characterized Uncle Will's home. They pitched horseshoes in the back yard, and many neighborhood kids often hung around. His two daughters, Stella and Pearl were very close to me in age as well as in likes, and had many friends at their home. In comparison to Aunt Mary's constant playing of Christian talk radio and gospel music, my Uncle

Will's home was more to my liking. Visiting his home became my reason for going to Norfolk, even after I received my discharge and returned home to Newark in 1974. I enjoyed the liveliness of his home and the friendship of his oldest daughter, Stella. I tried to keep in contact with them over the years.

When I went to college in Arizona in 1976 to study photography, I brought from home an old photography book that belonged to my father. One day when I opened the book, a letter postmarked in 1948 fell out. Its envelope carried a return address from somewhere in Brooklyn, New York belonging to another of my mother's brothers, Clifton. Out of curiosity, I sent a letter to that address, but it came back as undeliverable.

Upon returning home following that semester, I spoke to my father about the letter from my uncle. He remembered Clifton, but believed no one heard from him since the late 1940's. He said Clifton once lived on Kosciuszko Street in Brooklyn and had many children. The information my father provided fueled my desire to find out more about this portion of the family. It also added to my turmoil since Newark, New Jersey is only a stone's throw away from Brooklyn, New York. Now I knew there were cousins from my mother's side of the family in close proximity, but I never met any of them.

Another incident sparked my interest in my mother's family while I worked on library research paper for a class. I stumbled on to an autobiography of a Black Congressman, John Mercer Langston from Virginia, who served in the

U.S. House of Representatives after the Reconstruction period. According to this 1896 book, his Langston surname differed from his Caucasian father, Ralph Quarles. Quarles married an emancipated slave mistress named Lucy Langston, who came from "out of the swamp". Also according to the autobiography, her Langston surname came from Indian origin. They produced many children, all of them keeping the Langston surname, and becoming the property of Quarles. Upon his death, the children received their freedom as an act of Quarles' will. The female heirs divided the huge property holdings amongst themselves, while the two sons were sent to school in Ohio.

I tried to find a connection between this family and my mother's, but as of yet have failed to do so. Perhaps the Langston surnames John Mercer and my mother share is a coincidence, although I found Lucy Langston is a name that repeats often in my mother's family. But another coincidence exists. The swamp his mother came from is located in the same area along the Virginia-North Carolina border where my mother's family hails. I filed this research information away for later study.

For several years, I was unable to visit my Uncle Will and Aunt Mary. I lost touch with them following my last visit to Norfolk in the late summer of 1980. Shortly thereafter I relocated back out west to Arizona. In September 1985, my mother died, and I returned to New Jersey to live. That same month, my cousin Liz from Philadelphia also died, and her only son Tony moved to Norfolk to care for my Aunt Mary, his grandmother. His drinking and drug use caused her to lose her home, and she had to move in with my Uncle Will and his wife.

It took a few years to get into looking into my family roots again. I came across a copy of my mother's birth certificate that gave the names of her parents. I don't ever remember knowing their names before reading the certificate. Then in the late 80's, I found one of my old address books with my Uncle Will's address and telephone number. I called him to learn my Ant Mary lived in a nursing home suffering from blindness and Alzheimer's and my Aunt Dot was receiving dialysis.

In early 1989, I began asking Uncle Will about the Langston family. He told me information that included names of his aunts, uncles, some of his and cousins. He could not give me addresses or telephone numbers, but said a few of them still lived in Gates County, North Carolina. He mentioned the names of his half brother and sister Eugene and Nora, also living in Gates, but possessed little information about the lives of his two older brothers, Abraham and Clifton to give me.

I took a gamble and called directory assistance in Gatesville, a town in Gates County, trying to find a telephone number for my aunt or uncle. After speaking to the operator, she gave me several numbers to families with the surnames of Langston. I must have called about five different numbers before finally finding someone who could tell me something of what I wanted to know. That person was Daisy Langston Eure, who turned out to be my mother's first cousin.

After telling Daisy the name of my mother, it took only a second for her to start telling me what she knew. She gave me the names of her grandparents (my great-grandparents), Gaston and Lucy Langston, and most of their offspring. She told me of the offspring of her parents Emeline Billups and Willie Edgar Langston, both of whom lived extremely long lives. She also told me that their branch Langston family has a family reunion each year and that her daughter Daisy (who lives in Newark coincidentally) was one of the organizers.

I was shocked. My mother's second cousin had several children, and lived in my home town, not far from where I grew up. I made telephone contact with the younger Daisy and as we talked, she gave me more information about my great grandfather Gaston Langston, his offspring, and his offspring's children than I could digest at one time. She seemed just as excited to make this family connection, and sent me information about the family's next reunion. Along with the letter and flyer for the reunion, she sent a brochure with a brief narrative of the family history.

I was unable to make it to the annual reunion that year. My work schedule made planning for it difficult, as did my financial situation. By the time I attempted to contact the younger Daisy again, she had moved back down to Gates County. I passed the reunion information on to my brothers and sisters, but none of them made it to the reunions either.

The family history information Daisy sent me raised more questions than it answered in my mind. Some of the dates

103

listed in the brochure seemed to contradict my knowledge of history (my college major). How could my great-grandfather Gaston have come to America on a slave ship directly from Africa? How old was he when he came to America and when did it happen? Where did his name Gaston come from, especially since it is far more common in French than English? Could he have come from Haiti (an independent Black French speaking nation) instead of Africa? Did he come to America as a slave or as a free man? How long could he have been a slave, since the Civil War ended in 1865? Since all evidence pointed to him being married in the 1870's or 1880's, how old was he? I filed the information and questions away for another year.

Then in December 1992, I received a call from my cousin Pearl, telling me that Aunt Dot passed on. For the first time since 1980, I found myself in Norfolk again. After the funeral, I made a commitment to visit again the way I used to do. Over the next year, I kept that promise.

In reestablishing my relationships with my Uncle Will's family, I came to find that Stella and Pearl were my Aunt's children, but not my uncle's offspring. I guess I always knew, but did not care. Within that year, my father died and in early 1994 so did my Uncle Will. It was after his death that I renewed my search for my Langston roots.

My Aunt Nora (my mother's half sister) came to the funeral along with two of her three daughters. If I met Nora before I did not remember her. She looked so much like my Aunt Mary and her daughter Liz. It was the first time I had met my cousins. I took their addresses down and said

I would contact them. They did not seem very interested in improving family contact.

I continued to make a few trips to Norfolk over the next year. On one of those visits, I made one brief journey to Gates County. It was the first time I had been there since I was very young. I went there with one of my cousin's Stella's sons, Darryl. We lacked a map, but entered the town of Gatesville a little after nightfall. I found a payphone with a telephone book, and called Daisy Eure.

Daisy was surprised to hear from me, and gave directions to her front door. Upon arriving, the younger Daisy welcomed us and took me to her mother next door. We spoke for a short time then she called another of our kinfolk, Sara Hurdle, on the telephone. Sarah knew exactly who I was. She relayed a story about me falling in the mud on her farm when I was about four years old. After about an hour of family fellowship, I returned to Norfolk feeling very satisfied. When I got home to Newark I called my sister Michelle to tell her about my escapade into Gates County. She seemed very excited to hear about the journey. I filed the search for about a year after our conversation.

In February 1996, my Aunt Mary died. During that summer, my wife and I took a short driving vacation to Norfolk to visit my cousin Stella and her children, and to Gates County to look up my Uncle Eugene or Nora. I searched for other of the Langston surname in the phone book, talked to complete strangers, and tried to retrace the steps to Daisy's home. After a very frantic hour of being lost, someone directed me to Fannie Langston, who was a third grade teacher at the local school. Fannie married into the Langston family. She gave me directions to Daisy's home.

We arrived at Daisy's door but no one was home. (I learned later she was taken to the hospital that very morning.) At this point, I was flabbergasted when from the other side of the road I heard someone asking if he could help me. I do not remember his name, but he gathered we were cousins in one way or another. Once I told him who I was looking for, he rode with my wife and I directly to my Uncle Eugene's trailer. I finally got a chance to meet my uncle. The visit was short but gratifying.

In June 1997, something changed how I was going about my search. I purchased a computer, my first, and bought access to the Internet. I found that one of the things I could do was look up addresses and phone numbers. Remembering the time I had the year before trying to connect with my Uncle Eugene, I printed up the Langston and Eure listings from Gates County.

Then I did some exploring, and the first place I looked at was Brooklyn, New York. To my surprise I found a listing for one Clifton Langston, the same name as one of my mother's missing brothers. Another place I looked was Waterbury, Connecticut where I hoped to find the listing of my mother's first cousins, Miles Gaston Langston.

On the Fourth of July, I took a chance to visit these people, unannounced. I got off the subway a few short blocks from the Brooklyn address and walked the remaining distance. Two blocks from the street I was looking for, I passed Kosciuszko Street. It excited me to find the street name from the old letter I once discovered so close to my eventual destination. When I arrived at the address I sought, two older Black men were sitting outside, drinking beer and talking. I asked for Clifton Langston and the younger of the two responded.

From what I knew, my mother's brother Clifton was older than she and would have been in his eighties. This gentleman was in his fifties, but we talked anyway. It turned out his father who died in the early 1950's was also named Clifton, and his family lived on Kosciuszko Street for a long time. He knew nothing about his father's side of the family yet had always wanted to know about it. Then I introduced myself as his first cousin, and told him what I could. He was overjoyed. Family had found family.

Clifton told me his brothers' and sister' names, I knew the family connection was real. There are many names in the family I found that repeat, and his siblings had them too. It was hard to contain my enthusiasm. My cousin spoke about his father's death by alcoholism, and the deaths of his brother, sister, oldest daughter. He also spoke of his living siblings, his children, and grandchildren. He gave me the best information he could including the phone number of his mother, who had remarried and was living in New Jersey within a few miles of a couple of my sisters.

Happy does not describe how I felt when I discovered Clifton that day. I had found a whole branch of the family that no one had talked to in over forty years. I felt very proud of myself and could not wait o spread the word.

I then took the train from Grand Central Station to Waterbury. When I arrived, I found the listing I had was out-dated, and no one I asked could tell me where I would find a person by the name of Langston. I took the last train home, and chalked up the day as a victory.

The next evening I called my sister Michelle to tell her what I had found and she was amazed. The following morning I called Clifton's sister and mother, both named Esther and talked to them for awhile. When I first got my cousin Esther on the phone, she was half-asleep. I began by asking her questions about what she knew about her father's family, and she became very suspicious to say the least. But when I explained to her exactly who I was, she became quite inquisitive herself. I said I would send them the information I had on the family thus far. They both seemed very enthusiastic.

Then I called one of my cousins in Virginia, my Aunt Nora's daughter named Chineta. She did not seem very interested in the discovery of first cousins living in New York, but she gave me the phone number of a gentleman named James Sears and suggested that I call him. I was confused but followed her directions anyway.

With the one phone call to James a whole generation and the origin of the surname Langston was given to me. I could now trace my ancestry back to my great-great grandfather on my mother's side of the family, back to

Jamaica. It seems my great grandfather Gaston Langston was born in Jamaica as Gaston Sears. His parents were Jerry and Priscilla Sears. I knew now that my great-grandfather was born a free man, and was stolen into slavery.

Still there seemed to be a lot of information that was missing. The key to the information seemed to lie with a distant cousin, Miles Gaston Langston who lived somewhere in Waterbury, Connecticut. His name was first given to me by my uncle Will. No one seemed to be able to give me a phone number for him though.

I began looking over the old family reunion flyers, and called some of the contact people listed. I had a little luck speaking to some people in Gates County, but a lot seemed to fall into place when I called Agnes Langston Griffin. She is a great-niece of my grandfather, and provided me with enough information to have a connection to a large segment of the Langston family that left Gates County for Waterbury, Connecticut.

Over the course of the 1997 summer, I made several long calls o Waterbury and the Gates County vicinity. I finally contacted surviving members of my mother's first cousins, and their offspring. I made another visit to Waterbury, and finally met some of the people I had spoken to on the phone.

And yes, they thought there must be something wrong with me for me to go unannounced into new areas to find unknown family members.

Now in 1998, I'm on the threshold of attending a Langston Family Reunion in Waterbury over the Fourth of July weekend. It is my first, and hopefully not the last.

Reaction Paper #3 for Music 117

It was the night of February 28, 1975, and I was exposed to the kind of performance that I had vowed not to witness. It wasn't a show, but a wake for my grandfather's brother. Since I never knew my grandfather, I felt obliged to attend his brother's funeral. At his wake, I found out that he was a member of a free Black Mason order and that they hold their own kind of service at wakes of their members. This was my musical experience, a ceremony for the dearly departed, and the singing of spirituals that would suit the occasion.

The media was vocal, without instrumental accompaniment, and the performers were all the members of that lodge of Masons. The wake was a solemn affair and one seemed to feel that the performers felt the mood of the event. When the performers had to recite certain biblical passages, they seemed to be choked by the ones which gave impressions of my great-uncle. This conveyed to me that the performers were sincere in their grief from the loss of their friend and lodge brother. This was a mutual feeling with the audience, but as to the conveyance of these emotions was the singing of the spirituals.

The spirituals were based more so on emotion than on structure. There was no smooth blending of voices for the performers were not interested in such trivia. They all recited the words in their natural keys and the resulting sound was what I might describe as sincere and solemn, but natural and keeping with the mood of the occasion.

The atmosphere for the performance was strange for me because I have never been able to sit through such an occasion before. Everyone in the audience was family members, some of whom had not seen other members of the congregation in years. No one in reality seemed to expect the service but when the Masons came in humming, "This May Be the Last Time", everyone took a sea and became apprehensive. When all became quiet after the Masons had lined up, the service began with a short eulogy and biography of David Cook. The audience soon began to show their remorse, whereas a few moments before the area seemed as festive as any family reunion could get. I am not a religious man and would not be caught up in wakes and funerals normally, but I was really moved. After the performance, I went to pay my respect to my kin. All I could do was stare at the man that was the subject of the performance. I think for the first time in a very long time, I grieved over the death of a person with sincerity

There were times in the past when I had to listen to a choir or chorus that performed spiritual music. It was all very commercial and nothing was gained by my presence. Certain church groups sing spirituals also, but I could never seem to get the spirit, or to be moved in any way by such a performance. What I saw and heard at the wake was closer to the heart, and I caught something that seems to stick. It wasn't the spirituals whose words I forgot almost immediately, but the purity of mood that I felt around me during and after the Masons let their presence be known and their emotions felt by all.

A Letter To My Father For Christmas
Originally written in December 1979
(on a brown paper bag)

In May of this year, we of the Cook family suffered a great loss. My grandmother, your mother passed on to be nearer to God in peaceful sleep with those who came and left before her. You have been after me for a while to write something about her, kind of like what I did for Uncle Dave's wake. I did that piece for a class, and maybe you want something more about Momma. This is not her life story for I am not qualified to tell it, but please still allow me this testimonial.

There are a few things I know. Your father died when you were young, and that left Momma to raise her minions alone. Momma had a lot of kids, and I think all but Uncle Buddy had kids. Many of your brothers and sisters lived close to Momma, and their kids were always close at hand. She suffered the loss of a daughter, and raised that grandchild, Darryl, from infancy, and Ronnie lived with her there in Braddock until he was about 18 years old too.

I feel at a disadvantage. We were raised more than 400 miles away from Braddock and that solid core of the Cook family. Most of our exposure to Momma came maybe once a year when we would visit for a week, or when she came to Newark and made the rounds of all her relations in our part of the world. Even during our visits there, I spent more time around my many cousins, aunts and uncles who had the privilege of living so close to Momma. I only ran to her house when Ronnie chased me there or when it was time to eat. Despite the distance we lived apart, or the reason I ran to her home, Momma always welcomed me. Even when you and Mother stopped living together, she still always visited us at Mother's house. She loved us…she loved us all.

I remember one night a few years ago when I was traveling by bus back to school, I arrived in Pittsburgh at about 2:00 a.m. and had a few hours to layover. I called Momma, and you should've known she was glad to hear from me. But not only that, she made arrangements for me to get into Braddock if only for a few minutes to rest, relax, and recuperate before my long journey continued.

Momma was kind to us all, but her kindness was not born out of weakness, nor can be confused with such. She was strong, but she had to be in order to raise her children, many of her grandchildren, and even a few of her great-grandchildren in this world that was not of her making. She demanded respect from all of us. When she called us, we answered with "Yes Mamn," and when she said "Stop that fussing" there'd be need for nothing else. Above all though, she loved us…she loved us all.

A lot of people came to Momma's funeral. I remember the minister saying before entering the church for family to enter first, then friends, and finally church members. I remember having to stand outside as the church was overflowing from just family members alone. Not only were there her children, grandchildren, and great-grandchildren, but also some sisters and brothers, cousins and more. She was loved by many, and she loved us all.

When I listened to the sermon over Momma, I knew they had the same person in mind, but already something was missing. She had religion, but in everyday life I saw not her work with those church groups the minister related to. If one of hers was ill, she tried to be there. When we visited her, you can count on grits for breakfast, always a little treat around the house, and dinner was excellent. But above all, she loved us. She showed it in more ways than with the bread she broke at her table, and more than her presence represented.

You were very close to your mother, a closeness I almost envy. I remember getting the news that Momma died not more than three minutes after you left out the house to take her a new dress for Mother's Day and her birthday. I remember running to catch you at Fisher's house. I remember catching the first bus to Pittsburgh and finding you stretched out on Momma's couch in complete shock and disarray. I never saw you like that before, not even the times I saw you near death in the hospital following one of your heart attacks. You drove 412 miles to visit your mother, to bring her a gift, only to find out she died before your journey started, and that gift was to become her burial gown. At her wake and funeral was the first time I ever saw you cry. The only other time I saw that was when Mother died.

The First Week of September Stress

I don't know who to say this to so I will say it to myself. Today is September 1, 2004, and once again I find myself lost about what to do and how to do it. It is a crisis for me, and I have felt this way before, always at this time of year.

This is the week that my mother died in 1985. This is the week I was diagnosed with hypertension in 1983. This is the week Jeanne moved out of our house in 1980, and again in 1998. More recently, it is the week that I left my job at East Orange General Hospital in 2002 to move to the desert. It is the month I signed the divorce papers in 2002. It is the week in that I left my job at Urban Renewal in 2001. It is the week I left my job at East Orange General Hospital in 1999. And right now for a few minutes I felt so frustrated at how things are working or not working for me that I felt like just leaving my job here a Chicanos Por La Causa.

There is nothing really so wrong here, the feeling is coming from within me. I normally do good work but the quality of my charting has never been worse, I argue about almost everything because it doesn't seem right or it doesn't move smoothly from one point to the next for me. I don't seem to be able to cope with what I am supposed to do anymore. I am very frustrated.

Clearly I am having a very hard time today, and I expect "The Beatings Will Continue Until Moral Improves".

The First Day of the Conversion

There usually comes a day in a man's life when he finds out that he has been fooling himself. For me, that day preceded a week of suffering, hunger, and mental anguish before I knew just what had been happening to me. It was the first day, now that I think about it that set the stage for the rest of my life. Two incidents occurred on that day haunts me to this day. The first involved the jumping cactus named Cholla, and the other was my seeing the face and hearing the voice of what I believe was that of God.

I was at the time staying with friends Rob and his wife Linda in Arizona. It was four or five days before Christmas, and I hoped to stay with them instead of going all the way across country for the semester break.

The day started like most other days, with my waking early, and with no concrete plans on how I would spend my conscious hours. It's the makings of a beautiful day. Rob and Linda left the house early this day to go to work. They left me there with Rob's cousin John and his wife.

After washing the sleep from my eyes and eating a light meal, I found myself just moping around the house. John asked me to join him and his wife, and a few other friends for a trip to the Saguaro Lake. It sounded like a good idea, and at least I wouldn't be left to myself. I agreed to go and packed my camera for the trip.

So, at about 8:30 in the morning, the three of us piled into the car and pulled out for Phoenix to pick up the others. We had a little stash with us, so we took a few pulls before we reached the friends' home. We blew some more smoke before we readied ourselves to leave for the mountains. Now there were five of us, with three crowded into the back of the Volkswagen Beetle. We were on our way.

Most of the trip there was quiet, and devoid of conversation. The car stereo blasted some rock and roll, but the music was merely an after effect. The panoramic vista changing from city life and desert land to rocky paradise took our breath away, as did a few more joints we passed around from time to time. After a short while, the conversation warmed up.

As we got closer to the lake's recreational area, and the song "Sneakin' Up Behind You" by the Brecker Brothers screamed out of the tape deck, something in the joints we smoked began to kick back. Te world became surreal. Colors, textures, content, and context kept changing. I began hearing things, imagining things and entertaining thoughts of love and power. I began snapping pictures of the people and he landscapes. I was looking for something.

We arrived at Saguaro Lake, a man-made reservoir and recreational watershed on the Salt River Valley at about 10:30. The sky was very clear blue, the weather seemed perfect, and we all felt quite nice. We jumped into the lake, walked along the sandy shore, ate, and smoke more herb.

John and I decided to take a hike up to the surprising steep top of a ridge above the lake, to chill out and enjoy the atmosphere. The further we trekked up the incline, the steeper it got until instead of walking, we were climbing hands first, on all fours. I reached up to grab hold of a ledge above my eyesight and the small round balls of cactus known as Cholla bit me.

The thorns from the cactus caused great discomfort because they stuck in my hands, and I could not work them out. When I tried to remove one of the sharply pointed, inch long, and spike like barbs from one hand, it stuck in the other. I bled only slightly, but damn it hurt. John's wife had to pull them out for me, one by one. It took what seemed like hours before she got them all out.

I felt bad because the accident put a damper on the nice high we had, and that we decided to leave the lake early. So as we dropped off the others in Phoenix I talked John into climbing the rise behind Sun Devil Stadium to cool out before finally calling it a day.

We made the climb on the run, which was an experience in itself, and reached the top winded. There we sat down and looked out towards Tempe Butte and South Mountain. It seemed so very quiet despite the approaching the evening rush hour. We heard only the sound of the wind going by our ears, and saw the sight of the sun moving towards the south and west. It was strange. Then suddenly, John and I just started talking, but not to each other.

I started by stating who I am, and who I thought I was. I spoke about being a part of the universe, created by God out of sand from the Earth. I envisioned myself moving forward in time, from the grain of sand that once stood atop of the Pyramids tip. I imagined that though time, the winds swept that same miniscule speck until it became a part of who I am, and where I am. I constantly repeated the words "I don't know, I don't know" as a four measure chant.

I couldn't hear what John was saying. I mean, I heard his voice but I couldn't understand his words despite the fact he was sitting down right next to me. What I remember was the sound of the breeze going by my eardrums with the impact of thunder, the gleam of sun reaching for the horizon, and the moment when John and I both ended our soliloquy. We looked at each other and knew it was time to come down off our highs.

I came down off the mount behind the stadium with a vision to go home to Jersey, and bring a young lady I knew with a particularly beautiful voice back to Arizona with me. Although I planned to stay in Arizona for the entire semester break, I bought bus tickets for a round trip back home right away. I thanked John and his wife for their friendship, and Rob and Linda for their hospitality, then boarded the Silver Dog to Newark.

For the next three days, I rode the bus and fasted. Black coffee and orange juice was my only sustenance during the entire trip. I did not eat solid food for almost four days, and sat up in the seat of the Greyhound bus, no getting very much sleep. I still felt high, higher than I ever felt before.

I couldn't explain it past what I saw, heard, and thought on top of that mount in Arizona. I arrived in Jersey early on

Christmas Day feeling strong and clear about my mission for being there.

I dropped m belongings at my mother's house, then went across the bridge to ask, no, to beg my friend to come back to Arizona with me. Her entire family was there. For what seemed like hours, expressed my undying affection. Everybody present must have thought I was crazy, and I must have been. But instead of ridiculing me, or calling the police, everyone from my friend's father to her youngest brother and sister heard me out. Her mother fed me, then sent me home, where I finally got some sleep. I woke up almost two full days later feeling very embarrassed.

When I took a shower, I noticed a red mark half way up my right thigh. I touched it and the center of the bruise was quite hard. Upon closer examination, I found a 1-1/2 inch cactus spur buried within my leg. It wasn't until later that I learned the spiny thorns of that kind of cactus may have poisoned me and caused a hallucinogenic effect. I never tried to explain that part of the story to anyone.

Dear Family, Brothers, & Friends:

This year, I lost my wallet three times. The first two times I got it back, intact. The third time, which was lost closest to home, it was gone forever. I lost my ID card I need to go to work twice. I got hit by a car and was so mad at the driver of the car, I did not stop long enough to get his license plate number. I had personal property taken from my office. My kindness has been taken as a weakness by a number of people whom I held close to my heart.

I have been laughed at, talked about, criticized, and disputed.

Up to one week ago, I was happy satisfied with where I was and what I was doing with my life when suddenly, the masks of trying to get along at work, and fear of rocking the boat in personal relationships for the sake of comfort was ripped away. I had an emotional epiphany. Anger and frustration took the place of the fake peace I had come to accept. I could not take it anymore. And in my heart I knew then it would never be the same again.

And I Said "Take This Job and Shove It"

And the people I work with, those of whom I respect very much echoed the lyrics of the Beatles song, "We Can Work It Out", because they also liked me and the qualities I brought to my work. They said I could take it, they said they would help me take it. And I said to them I could not take it, that I should not have to take it. They said take the time to think about it. But in my heart I knew then it could never be the same again.

I walked out, sat in the sun, and prayed for hours, within a two minute walk and straight line eyeshot of my place of employment. I saw them, I even was able to hear them, but they had no clue as to where I was. When the sun got to a point in the sky where I could not shield my eyes from its brightness, I began to walk. The first person came across was a person I had previously had the misfortune of being supervised by, a minister, addicted to women, money, and style. He shook my hand, and asked which direction I was going in. I could only think to say home, and he could only thing to say in his glib manner that he was going in a different direction.

I was not in a place that was a part of my routine, but I still got to my destination. And for 3 days, I made no attempt to contact anyone by sight or voice, and took no attempt by them for the same. I did contact someone electronically, who apologized to me for his part in my heated passions at work, and his desire to continue to work with me in our field of expertise. I thanked him for his concern, and told him he will be better in that field than I.

Go South Go West, Go Southwest.

I sat mesmerized by electronic screens, searching within their patterns of electrons for an answer, a direction. I had no plan to do this, I damn sure didn't have the resources for it. I as burdened by responsibilities here, relationships. It was safe here. I can make it here. I wasn't ready. I didn't know why I need to heed the call, except for I knew deep down inside I can't reach my greatest height until I do. My life depended on it.

I had to decide where. Two targets came up, Phoenix Arizona where I already have a very strong base of support, and New Mexico which was close to Phoenix, (relatively from where I stand now). The strongest pull comes from New Mexico so it is the primary goal with Phoenix becoming the fall back position.

Walk By Faith Not By Sight

I had to decide how to make the move successful. I began to pack my clothes, and making the decisions on what I can take, what I need to take, and of everything I would want to have with me. I knew I needed to shed many burdens here, find transportation, find a job where I am heading, get a place to live, and begin to say my good-byes. I gave myself 19 days to leave.

My first attempt to contact someone by voice was a friend who had asked me earlier this year to deliver a car to Phoenix. There was no longer a need to do this, but since I saw my friend as a true friend, I spoke of my dilemmas, my lack of resources, direction, job, and my needs to make the plan work. And all my friend could offer me was to say how happy I sounded with the decision I made.

Another friend from the job was able to contact me. He insisted I was letting people down, that I am not prepared for this journey, that I should stop to think about it, pray about it…and come back to the job where he had been working overtime in my absence.

I spoke to another friend two days ago, and I wondered if he had a spare laptop computer, since I had these two desktops to get rid of. He could not help me there, but he said he had a home for the houseplants I have been nurturing. He also said he did not want to see me go, but made no effort to hold me back.

Yesterday, I went to visit a friend as an after-thought. While waiting in his office for some free time to speak to him, I overheard his progress on his completion of a number of halfway houses for ex-offenders. So when I treated him to lunch, I told him of my dilemmas. He told me I should have planned this better; that I should be better prepared for such an undertaking. Then he told me he had a station wagon he no longer needed, and that I can expect him out there to visit. We struck a deal for the car.

I spoke to my brother, and told him of my dilemma and needs for car insurance. He said he would think about how he can help. In the meantime, I know I can use his address as mine locally, until I get set in my new locale. Late last night, I spoke to my other brother and we struck a deal for an IBM ThinkPad.

Today is my day of notifications. I will notify my job, return keys and identification, and arrange for my meager pension funds to be sent to my checking account. Today I will notify my landlord, and plan to turn over my keys and arrange for the return of my security deposit. Today I will notify the post office, utility company, the telephone company, and the cable company. Today I will notify my medical provider and arrange for an advance shipment of medications to last until I am settled. I will notify the local members of my dear Fraternity, at the last meeting I will have with this Chapter.

And I will notify you my friends.

Post Script

I left Newark's city limits at twelve noon on that early autumn day, the first Thursday in October, driving west. Somehow I had enough cash for gas and some extras, a fully loaded Ford Taurus Wagon, and hoped it would all work out. That first night I stopped for a few hours of sleep in West Virginia, before going on to near Columbus, Ohio for more rest. I drove all day Friday through the rest of Ohio, Indiana, and Illinois. I believed I had picked up on my tail an unscrupulous road gang that seemed to follow me from a rest stop in Indiana where I stopped for a late breakfast all the way to the outskirts of St. Louis right at the evening rush hour. I lost them there.

I continued, driving southwest through Missouri that evening and most of that night, feeling excited because of my desire to reach Tulsa, Oklahoma to drop in on a very close friend I had not seen in almost twenty years. I took only a few short cat naps that night, driving whenever I would awake for an hour or so, before napping again. I arrived in Tulsa just around eight in the morning, and found Ivan's home by asking a few directions from a convenience store clerk.

To say the least, Ivan was surprised and happy to see me. He introduced me to his wife and children, then showed me around. It felt damned good to be out of the car for a little bit. I was treated to a home cooked meal made by his wife as we caught up with some old times. It was a good visit. We exchanged gifts, and our famed Brotherhood grip, and I was on my way again just before noon.

At Oklahoma City, I turned west again, driving through the panhandle of Texas, reaching Amarillo a little after nightfall, right in time for a dinner at a McDonalds. I set my goal to drive as far into New Mexico as I could that night. I think I made it a little more than a hundred miles in before pulling over and falling to sleep before midnight.

I ate breakfast the next morning in Albuquerque, and crossed into Arizona a little past noon. I stopped for lunch near a reservation, where I spoke to a few Navaho tribesmen, who spoke of the troubles concerning alcohol addiction amongst their people.

As I drove past Holbrook near the exit for the Crater National Park I had my first problem with the car, a blowout of the left rear tire. I pulled over, unloaded the packed down vehicle, pulled out a spare tire I knew I had, and changed the flat. I drove then to Flagstaff and south towards Phoenix.

I arrived at the city limits around 7:30 p.m., and knew of just one place to go, Rie's house. Rie has been a sister like

127

friend to me since we met at ASU in the mid seventies. We share the same birthday, and have kept in contact over those years. And besides, with her I would need no explanations about anything.

I got to her door at about 8 p.m. I rang her front door bell, and when she opened it I said something humorous like "hey lady, I'm lost. Can you help me out? Her reply, "George, what are you doing here? How did you get here, get in here!"

I told her my story, and my journey, and she gave me her spare room.

In four days I had a job, and on the fifth day my own place. All that happened within the thirty nine days from leaving my job at East Orange General Hospital, and nine days after getting in the Taurus and leaving my home in Newark, New Jersey. Seven months later, I purchased my first home. Twenty six months after that, I left my job at Chicanos Por La Causa, Inc for my current journey, to write.

Post Post Script

Three years has passed since the post script was written. My journey has taken me through the longest period of unemployment of my life, physical and mental depression, near foreclosure before selling my home for a small profit before the bubble burst, quasi homelessness, being as broke as a broke dick dog, and now to working in a field for which I have a few qualifications and no certification, the teaching of general music in an elementary school.

I guess after leaving CPLC, I thought my work experience should land me a job in no time. It didn't. I found myself devoid of interview possibilities in my field of expertise. And if I did get an interview, I would be promised a second with a higher up that never came. One company did hire me but pulled back the position because I could not pee on demand (and I had been clean for more than a decade). Obviously, God had other plans for me.

I began to fall behind in my bills since I was not receiving any unemployment benefits. I began sending out resumes in fields where I had interest but no experience, and yes, I received no interviews. I began getting depressed, especially after my water was cut off by the city when I missed two consecutive bills. A neighbor insured I had water though.

Self Portrait I

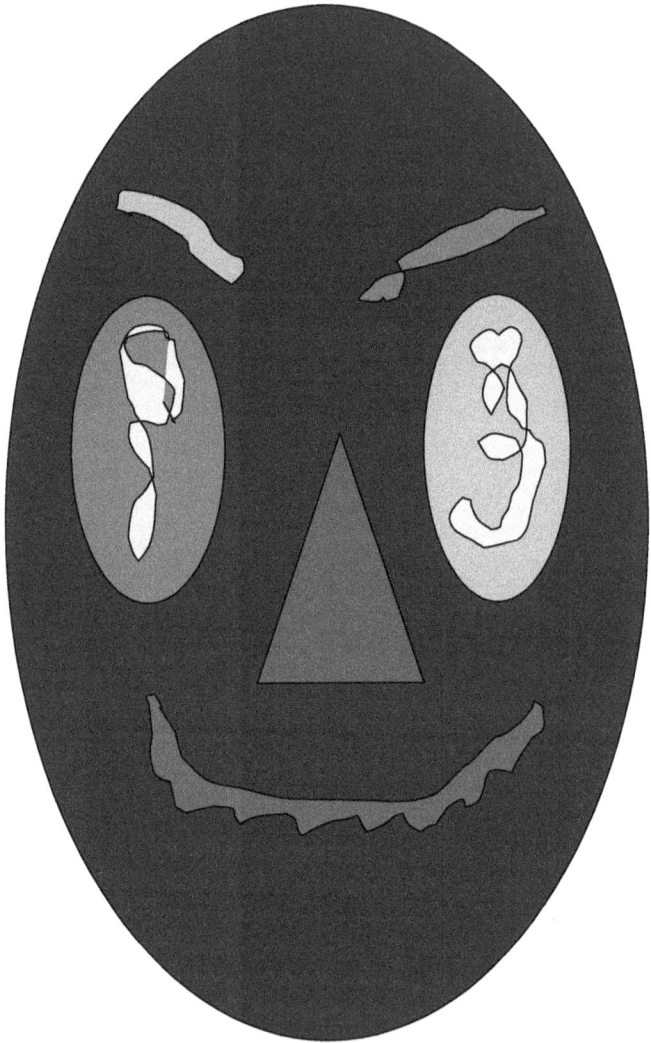

Self Portrait 2001

About the Author

George Langston Cook was born May 23, 1952 in Newark, New Jersey to George Henry and Lucy Mae Langston Cook. The third child and oldest son of this marriage's seven children, George was raised in the federal housing projects of Christopher Columbus Homes, and educated in Newark's public schools.

After graduating high school he entered the U.S. Navy during the Vietnam Era, where he began to photograph and write for his own pleasure. Upon his Honorable Discharge in 1974, George enrolled in Essex County College in Newark where earned an Associates Degree in Secondary Education. He gained some notoriety with his participation in student publication activities and before graduating with honors. He continued his education and student activities at Arizona State University, where he received his Bachelors of Science degree in History, and became a member of Alpha Phi Alpha Fraternity, Inc.

Mr. Cook has spent most of the last 25 years employed in Social Services, as a Teacher or a Substance Abuse Counselor in both Newark New Jersey and Phoenix Arizona. He has continued writing over that period.

www.ingramcontent.com/pod-product-compliance
Lightning Source LLC
Chambersburg PA
CBHW031852090426
42741CB00005B/460